THE ULTIMATE DETROIT TIGERS TIME MACHINE BOOK

THE ULTIMATE DETROIT TIGERS TIME MACHINE BOOK

MARTIN GITLIN

LYONS
PRESS

Essex, Connecticut

An imprint of Globe Pequot, the trade division of
The Rowman & Littlefield Publishing Group, Inc.
4501 Forbes Blvd., Ste. 200
Lanham, MD 20706
www.rowman.com

Distributed by NATIONAL BOOK NETWORK

British Library Cataloguing in Publication Information available

Library of Congress Cataloging-in-Publication Data

Names: Gitlin, Marty author.
Title: The ultimate Detroit Tigers time machine book / Martin Gitlin.
Description: Guilford, Connecticut : Lyons Press, [2022] | Includes
    bibliographical references.
Identifiers: LCCN 2021059704 (print) | LCCN 2021059705 (ebook) | ISBN
    9781493060559 (Paperback : acid-free paper) | ISBN 9781493068012 (ePub)
Subjects: LCSH: Detroit Tigers (Baseball team)—History. | Baseball
    players—Michigan—Detroit—History. |
    Baseball—Michigan—Detroit—History.
Classification: LCC GV875.D6 G57 2022 (print) | LCC GV875.D6 (ebook) |
    DDC 796.357/640977434—dc23/eng/20220119
LC record available at https://lccn.loc.gov/2021059704
LC ebook record available at https://lccn.loc.gov/2021059705

Contents

Contents

INTRODUCTION

It could have been any summer afternoon or evening in the mid- to late 1960s. I had either plopped myself on the orange and tan couch, which today would be considered hideous, in the den of my suburban Cleveland home for an Indians-Tigers game on TV or parked my skinny butt on the porch swing with transistor radio in hand. And this passionate Tribe fan who sometimes and, in retrospect, pathetically even cried after particularly galling losses would be on the verge of tears again.

I recall with vivid clarity those losing battles. No team exasperated Marty Gitlin the child and his team with greater frequency than the one local announcers called the Motor City Kitties. In my mind the scenario always felt achingly similar—taut battles into the ninth inning from which the Tigers emerged victorious because they knew how to win and the Indians were their patsies. Then came the anger and frustration, to which my father reacted with a lesson on perspective in life.

Of course, it did not always end that way. Sometimes Cleveland won. It just did not seem like it in the heart and mind of a child. I was too young to understand that Detroit was simply a superior club, one that through a higher level of talent, especially with bat in hand, outplayed its opponent. The names haunted the preteen me. Bill Freehan. Norm Cash. Al Kaline. Mickey Stanley. Willie Horton. Jim Northrup. While the club for which I rooted so deeply regularly failed to support a fine pitching staff with enough runs to win, the heart of the Tigers lineup remained steadfast and productive year after year. Such stalwarts brought peace of mind to rotation standouts Mickey Lolich, Denny McLain, and Earl Wilson. Their offensive capabilities gave the team an advantage in an era highlighted by 1–0 and 2–1 games so frequent and dull that Major League Baseball was motivated to lower mounds in 1969 to raise run totals. It was no wonder the Tigers of that period proved themselves the most consistent winner in the American League, one that brought joy and a sense of togetherness to the people of a beleaguered city, especially as their team steamrolled to the 1968 crown a year after one of the most devastating and deadly urban riots in American history.

Their existence has been marked neither by dynasties nor doldrums. The Tigers have captured just four World Series championships since becoming a charter member of the junior circuit in 1901. They compiled a record barely above .500 during that 120-year span. They have suffered through seasons of failure so pronounced that they have gone down as some of the worst in the annals of baseball. But their periodic years of greatness have proven so memorable that they have remained in the hearts and minds of Tigers fans forever. They have provided a sense of pride and optimism to even the most fervent and critical followers during the most woeful periods.

Then there are the individual stars who played significant roles in championship runs or performed so brilliantly that they will always be cherished by those who witnessed them in action or revered by those too young to have seen them play. They pepper Tigers history from the turn of the 20th century to today. Ty Cobb. The historically underappreciated Harry Heilmann and Charlie Gehringer. Hank Greenberg. Hal Newhouser. Kaline. Lolich. Alan Trammell and Lou Whitaker, whose names for good reason have most often been referenced together. Miguel Cabrera. Justin Verlander. Even flash-in-the-pan pitcher Mark Fidrych added color and fond memories. Tiger fans recall with relish where they were and how they felt during an otherwise unnoteworthy 1976 season when they watched "The Bird" talk to the baseball, mow down the opposition, and earn the focus of an entire nation.

This book covers the entirety of Tigers history and even delves into the birth of professional baseball in Detroit in the National League to its continuation in the Western League, which morphed into the American League. The following pages detail their greatest and most interesting teams, players, moments, and eras. Read about how Cobb transformed a poor club into a pennant winner yet emerged as one of the most universally hated and historically condemned players ever to don a baseball uniform for the irascible nature and competitive fire that made him downright dangerous on the basepaths. Learn how Heilmann excelled as one of the finest pure hitters in baseball and one of the most popular voices of the Tigers as the first player to serve as any team's play-by-play radio broadcaster. Gain insight into how Greenberg exploded onto the scene as the most prolific slugger to wear a Detroit uniform, then battled anti-Semitism at home and abroad.

This book details the postwar era and beyond, from Newhouser blossoming into the finest pitcher in franchise history and arguably remaining so after Lolich, Jack Morris, and Verlander came and went, to the tumultuous career of rebel-without-a-cause Denny McLain, to the impact of Sparky Anderson as perhaps the team's greatest manager ever, to a decade of misery wrapped around the launching of a new millennium, to the failures of aging owner Michael Ilitch to secure a World Series championship he so desired, to the collapse that followed.

It is all here—the saga of Detroit baseball. Enjoy.

CHAPTER ONE

Planting the Seeds

WILLIAM G. THOMPSON YEARNED TO DO MORE THAN SIMPLY ATTRACT a professional baseball team to Detroit in 1881. The mayor wanted to own it as well. He got his opportunity when the woeful Cincinnati Reds disbanded after angering league officials by selling beer and renting out their ballpark on Sundays. That left an opening in the National League that Thompson and his fledgling Wolverines filled. The nickname was adopted two decades after it had been first embraced at the University of Michigan.

Thompson believed the city, whose population had soared over 123,000 in 1880, had grown populous enough to support a major-league team, which was born two decades before the Tigers became a founding member of the American League. Its citizens had already shown an interest in the newfangled sport decades earlier. A group of wealthy folks bored with cricket formed a baseball team in 1858. They practiced diligently before playing the first game in city history on the grounds of a local farm on August 8, 1859, against a team of clerks and office workers that nicknamed themselves the Early Risers. It was no contest. The latter was smoked in an ERA-destroyer, 59–21.

The owner figured that Detroit proved itself worthy of a franchise in May 1879 when a team of Eastern players called Hollinger's Nine set up residence at Recreation Park on the corner of Brush and Brady Streets and lost to a team from Troy, New York, before 1,500 patrons occupying the wooden stands.

Wolverines manager Frank Bancroft, a Massachusetts hotel owner and late arrival into the world of baseball who guided the 1880 Worcester Ruby Legs to a 40-43 finish in his only year as a skipper, boasted little experienced hitting or pitching talent. The roster of his new club was dotted with castoffs and rookies. But they performed above expectations. They debuted with a 6-5 loss to Buffalo in front of 1,286 fans. A 3-10 start knocked them out of the pennant race permanently, but they recovered to finish 41–43, spurred by the fine performances of catcher Charlie Bennett, first baseman Martin Powell, and outfielder George Wood, all of whom sported typical-of-the-era moustaches and spearheaded a painfully young lineup that featured only one player older than 26.

Among the Kiddie Korps was 20-year-old pitcher Stump Weidman, who gained the nickname from his 5-foot-7, 165-pound frame. Weidman led the National League with a 1.80 earned run average. But the club required little pitching depth—rookie George Derby started and completed 55 games in compiling a 29-26 record and strong 2.20 ERA.

Those who thought the promising inaugural season destined the Wolverines to greatness had another think coming. They raised hopes the following year with a 25-14 start that placed them atop the standings before collapsing. A six-game losing streak in late August doomed them to a fifth-place finish as neither Derby nor Weidman performed to expectations and the downfall of Powell weakened the offense considerably. The .230 team batting average ranked last in the league.

Rampant gambling that permeated the sport cost the team dearly early that year. Umpires during that era were assigned to specific teams to cut down on travel costs. Shady ump Dick Higman was quite unfortunately appointed to the Wolverines. Thompson grew angry over several questionable calls during a stretch of struggles in late May and early June. The owner even hired a private investigator to shadow Higman. The sleuth intercepted a note from the umpire to gambler James Todd encouraging him to bet on Wolverine opponents. Thompson displayed the correspondence to fellow National League owners along with a handwriting sample of Higman to prove guilt. The umpire received a permanent ban before, appropriately, becoming a bookie in Chicago.

The defeats likely caused by such dishonesty could not excuse that midseason collapse nor the downfall that began before a game was played the next year when Bancroft bolted to manage the Cleveland Blues (then led the Providence Grays to the championship in 1884). Replacement Jack "Death to Flying Things" Chapman, whose greatness tracking down baseballs as an outfielder during his playing days earned him the colorful nickname, proved himself far less proficient as a manager.

His 1883 club rolled merrily along into early June with a 15-9 record before an epic downfall spurred by a pitching collapse. The Wolverines surrendered an average of 9.5 runs per game during a 2-19 stretch, then allowed a ridiculous 93 runs in a six-game period in the midst of a 1-14 run in August and September. They hit bottom in a September 6 loss to Chicago, yielding a league-record 18 runs in one inning en route to a 26–6 defeat.

That season, however, was a picnic compared to 1884. Thompson foolishly released Powell, who had remained one of the club's most productive hitters and rebounded to bat .319 for the Cincinnati Outlaw Reds of the American Association before retiring. But little could anyone have imagined the utter feebleness of the Detroit offense, which featured three starters with batting averages of .177 or lower and ranked last in the league in runs scored, on-base percentage, and strikeouts, nor the struggles of Weidman, who finished with a disturbing 4-21 mark. "Ace" Frank Meinke also exceeded 20 losses, more a victim of a lack of run support than poor performance.

There was no pretense of respectability for the Wolverines that year. They showed immediately why they would emerge as one of the worst teams in baseball history by falling to 1-15 out of the gate and embarking on two 11-game losing streaks, then outdoing themselves with runs of 0-12 and 0-9 in August and September to finish 28-84.

So much for Chapman. The revolving door at the managerial position was about to spin faster. Thompson hired player-manager Charlie Morton, who had the previous year played the same role with Toledo of the American Association. That move bombed when the 1885 Wolverines dropped an absurd 28 of 30 in May and June after a 3-0 start and surrendered double-figure runs in 12 of those games.

But Morton made one prudent move before moving on in favor of fellow one-time AA manager Bill Watkins. He granted a tryout to outfielder Sam Thompson, then signed him a week before his firing. Thompson sparked the Wolverines by sparking the offense. The club embarked on a 12-1 tear and averaged nearly seven runs per game in the process. Detroit fell apart again, but one could not blame Thompson, who emerged immediately as its premier hitter, leading the team in batting average and home runs despite his late arrival.

THOMPSON, RIGHT FIELD, DETROIT.

Sam Thompson emerged as the first star of the franchise.
COURTESY OF THE LIBRARY OF CONGRESS

The Hall of Famer blossomed into the team's first star. But he required help to transform the Wolverines into a contender, let alone a champion. And he received plenty—thanks to new owner Frederick Kimball Stearns, son of wealthy drug manufacturers, as well as a musician who founded the Detroit Orchestral Association, which morphed into the Detroit Symphony Orchestra. Stearns succeeded in transforming the Wolverines into a juggernaut by purchasing the Buffalo Bisons and "demoting" them into a minor-league team while commandeering their premier players. Included were first baseman Dan Brouthers, shortstop Jack Rowe, third baseman Deacon White, and outfielder Hardy Richardson. The emergence of unusually nicknamed pitchers Lady Baldwin and Pretzels Getzien, a German immigrant, finally provided a dominant one-two pitching punch.

The overhauled Wolverines displayed their dominance in 1886 by embarking on a 15-0 blitz in May and remaining on a roll. They won 12 of 13 during a June tear and 15 of 16 at the end of July to forge 4½ games ahead in the National League pennant race. There was just one problem, and they resided in Chicago. Detroit finished 87-36, but that only earned it the distinction of being the best second-place club in National League history. The Wolverines lost twice in the Windy City in late September to doom their title hopes. But their newcomers had transformed them into a powerhouse. Thompson, Brouthers, and Richardson led an offense that scored an incredible 315 more runs than it had the year before while the dynamite mound duo combined to win 72 games.

Both faded in 1887, but it mattered not because the Wolverines bludgeoned foe after foe with their bats. They averaged an outrageous 7.8 runs per game and led the league in batting average, doubles, triples, on-base percentage, and slugging percentage. Though they received a scare from Philadelphia and Chicago, they snagged the momentum with a 19-2 start and led the National League wire-to-wire. A 19-4 blitz in August and September put away the competition and set up a pre–World Series World Series against the American Association champion St. Louis Browns. The event in that era was more a barnstorming exhibition than a real battle for a crown—it did not even end when the Wolverines pulled too far ahead to be caught. They won the series of games 10-5 with Thompson emerging as its star by batting .362.

That success did not motivate fans to besiege Recreation Park. The lack of attendance and increased payroll placed the franchise in dire straits financially. Stearns could not afford the talent he procured from Buffalo and was forced to disband the Wolverines after a fifth-place finish in 1888.

Professional baseball in Detroit was no more. But it returned six years later when a new club joined a circuit that would eventually become the American League.

CHAPTER TWO

The Tigers before Ty

IT WAS APRIL 1885. GROVER CLEVELAND HAD BEEN SWORN IN AS THE 22nd president of the United States. Mark Twain had published *The Adventures of Huckleberry Finn*. The Detroit Wolverines were seeking a rebound from one of the worst seasons in baseball history. And the Western League was born. The new circuit proved unsteady. Franchises came and went from one year to the next. It died in 1892, sparked hope of a revival the following May, then folded again a month later. Any hope of a revival rested upon the luring of a strong leader.

Enter Ban Johnson. The passionate baseball fan eschewed the wishes of his parents that he enter the ministry to attend law school at the University of Cincinnati, then followed his heart to join a local newspaper as sportswriter and editor. The driven and outspoken Johnson expressed his opinions for the *Commercial Gazette* with vigor. He decried Red Stockings owner John T. Brush for what he perceived as placing profits ahead of the best interest of the sport. So annoyed was Brush that the executive, along with Red Stockings manager and future Hall of Famer Charles Comiskey, pushed for Johnson to put down his poison pen and become president of the reborn Western League.

Brush made certain Johnson got off his back by landing the job. Johnson then set out to give the new minor league a moral foundation he believed the National League lacked. He yearned to rid baseball of dirty play, as well as verbal and physical abuse of umpires. He decried rampant cheating in the National League such as infielders hiding baseballs in the grass and using them when needed. The rowdy behavior had grown so pronounced that women and children felt compelled to stay home, thereby weakening team attendance and revenue. Johnson succeeded in creating a clean, fan-friendly atmosphere while earning respect along the way that would eventually result in him becoming the most powerful leader in the sport.

It was in that environment that Detroit started its new affiliation with the professional game, though it had yet to adopt the Tigers as its nickname. The new club was owned by 29-year-old George Vanderbeck, whose family had gained wealth in various enterprises near Rochester, New York. He eventually married and moved to the West Coast, where he first owned the Portland team of the Pacific Northwest League and Los Angeles club of the California League. He was expelled from the latter in 1892 for shady dealings before gaining ownership of the fledgling Detroit franchise. Vanderbeck signed eight players from the California League, including manager and second baseman Bob Glenalvin. The owner bragged that the roster was filled with the "cream of the Pacific coast," inspiring the Detroit Creams nickname from the local press.[1] They were also dubbed the Giants in the belief they were the tallest team in the Western League.

How the permanent "Tigers" moniker was born has been the subject of debate for more than a century. One belief is that it was provided by the *Detroit Free Press* in its coverage of an exhibition game on April 16, 1895. Another is that it honored a local Civil War detachment that fought with such ferocity that it became known as the Tigers.

Vanderbeck did not live up to Johnson's ideals. Not only did his club flirt with the cellar but he engaged in a public dispute with infielder Monte Cross that resulted in a fight in the team offices on June 18. Cross asked for his release but was instead fined and suspended. He eventually landed in the major leagues, where he remained as a no-hit, good-fielding shortstop for 13 years. Vanderbeck then started a battle with *Free Press* sports editor and team official scorer Frank Cooke for perceived overcritical coverage. The owner lambasted all baseball reporters in Detroit and threatened to withhold information from them and give it instead to the *Toledo Blade*.

"Properly run the present team can play pretty good ball, but there is a demand for a change," offered the *Free Press* after the Creams finished with a 57-69 record. "Baseball has regained life here, and a good team will make the game popular and very profitable. If we cannot have National League ball give us a good article of minor league variety, not another season like the past."[2]

Vanderbeck could not stay out of trouble. He was accused of dispatching outfielder Howard Earle to umpire games played by rival Grand Rapids while still under contract with Detroit. Glenalvin claimed that the owner owed him $800 in salary and had created rifts with his players through the 1894 season. The manager prepared for war with Vanderbeck, stating that the latter would be happy to sell the team once all the truths had been revealed. Among them was an incident in which Vanderbeck reportedly released outfielder Jim Burns while on a train from Kansas City to Detroit, then left him stranded in Missouri with no money for a fare back to Detroit. The league soon ruled that Vanderbeck owed Burns his full salary and that if he refused the franchise would be revoked. He paid up, then angrily sold Glenalvin to Indianapolis.

"One thing that struck me forcibly was the perfect unanimity with which the Western League magnates don't like their Detroit colleague—Vanderbeck," wrote W. A. Phelon Jr. in *the Sporting Life*. "[He] has been responsible, so they say for 90 percent of all the league's troubles and difficulties; he has been invariably turned down, and yet keeps on troubling."[3]

The Tigers fared little better on the field than their owner did off it. New manager Con Strouthers guided them to another sub-.500 finish in 1895. Vanderbeck did move the franchise forward by purchasing property on the corner of Michigan and Trumbull for the construction of Bennett Park, which was named after popular former Wolverines catcher Charlie Bennett. No longer would the team be forced to play at cramped, rectangular Boulevard Park, which proved wholly inadequate for baseball. The new field, built at the site that would eventually house Tiger Stadium, opened in time for the 1896 season. Its convenient location allowed fans working or residing downtown to reach their destination in five minutes by streetcar.

The venue neither helped Vanderbeck behave nor transformed his team into a contender under journeyman manager George Stallings, who continued to bounce around from Detroit to Philadelphia after replacing Strouthers. The Tigers did eke over the .500 mark in three of the next four years but never finished closer than 10 games out of first place. Vanderbeck, meanwhile, continued to make enemies. The league threatened to expel him, then fined him $100 for player tampering in 1897. Indianapolis owner W. F. C. Golt accused him of artificially reducing player salaries. When cigar manufacturer William Gordon complained that foul balls struck in Bennett Park were damaging his plants and endangering his customers, Vanderbeck gained revenge by leasing his property and doubling the rent. An angry Gordon grabbed two foul balls and refused to return them to the team, which prompted the owner to accuse him of theft, resulting in imprisonment.

Despite his team's mediocrity Vanderbeck remained unsatisfied with its status as a minor-league organization. He attempted to lure away the National League franchises in Cleveland and Louisville to no avail. Johnson responded by claiming Western League territorial rights in Detroit and citing needed approval by both the NL and WL to legalize any such transaction.

The malcontented owner continued to flout the rules. He tried to withhold payment for two players he purchased from the Canadian League in 1899. The Tigers certainly could have used the help. They had bottomed out at 50-87 the previous season before the return of Stallings contributed to a 64-60 record that year. The manager also did Vanderbeck a favor by straightening his nose with a pencil after it had been socked by *Free Press* sports editor Moulton Needham, who had been stiffed his $300 fee for toiling as the team's scorekeeper.

Such incidents were typical of Vanderbeck. His abuse was not limited to those in his professional life, and he soon received his comeuppance in the form of a settlement with second wife, Mary, in June 1899. She was granted a divorce on grounds of adultery and cruelty when the court ruled after an investigation that her husband "consorted constantly with lewd women."[4] He was ordered to pay her the then whopping alimony sum of $8,000. He complained that such an outlay would wreck him financially, leading the court to place in receivership the Tigers, their ballpark, and rights to all the players while scheduling an auction that finally transpired in mid-February 1900.

What the many haters of Vanderbeck considered to be a delicious result of the proceedings outside Detroit City Hall was that Mary, the only bidder, bought the whole shebang for $9,500 while her ex watched with dismay from across the street. George appealed to the Michigan Supreme Court in vain. The action put franchise ownership into an indeterminate state and threatened the future of Tigers baseball. But Johnson quickly and emphatically cited the league expulsion of George Vanderbeck, stating that he would have no team to own even if the court ruled in his favor.

That league was no longer the minor-league Western League. Johnson was the commissioner of what was now the American League, which was pursuing major-league status that he and the owners hoped would allow it to compete with the established National League for fans and premier talent. The legal issues in Detroit threatened to ruin his plans. So he planned to move the franchise to Louisville if the legal wrangling remained unsettled.

The savior proved to be former amateur boxer and saloon owner James D. Burns. After Vanderbeck continued to take legal action against the auction, his ex-wife agreed to sell the club to Burns and Tigers player-manager George Stallings for $12,000. The transaction saved baseball in Detroit. But the stormy, tumultuous tenure of Vanderbeck as owner would remain troubling in the hearts and minds of all who were negatively affected. His legacy was encapsulated in the following opinion offered by the *Sporting Life*:

> *After having aired his affairs in the papers for many weeks and tried in every way to defeat his wife in her attempts to secure alimony, he is no longer a magnate. Had he taken the advice of his friends and not tried to beat his wife out of everything, or had he acted fairly and kept a few of the promises which he made, he could have settled his domestic affairs and might still own the Detroit Club and franchise. Now he is out, and among the other American League magnates there will be no regrets, for he was thoroughly disliked and distrusted.*[5]

THE DETROIT TIGERS OF 1900
DETROIT'S ENTRY INTO THE NEWLY
FORMED AMERICAN LEAGUE

Jones		Casey		Yager	Frisk	Shaw	McAllister		Holmes	Owens
	Sheehan		Harley							
Nicol		Ryan		Dillon	James D. Burns Pres.		George Stallings Mgr.		Seivers	Cronin

The 1900 Tigers of the fledgling American League
COURTESY OF WIKIMEDIA COMMONS

The Vanderbeck Era was in the rearview mirror when the American League opened for business in 1901. The opportunity for the Western League to take that step toward equality arrived when the National League contracted in 1899 by dumping the Baltimore, Cleveland, Louisville, and Washington franchises. Johnson wasted no time. During a special meeting, he proclaimed the birth of the American League along with the additions of teams in Cleveland and Chicago. A salary cap of $2,400 established by the senior circuit resulted in top talent scurrying to the American League. Johnson bolstered sagging franchises through financial backers. The new organization quickly bypassed the old one in popularity, drawing a half-million more fans by 1902.

That served the Tigers quite well as they clawed through the competition in their inaugural season. They certainly started with a bang before an estimated 8,000 fans at Bennett Park, coming from behind with a 10-run ninth inning to stun the Milwaukee Brewers. First baseman Pop Dillon played hero with four doubles, including a two-run game-winner.

A powerless era in baseball required teams to compile high on-base percentages and steal their way toward the plate. The 1901 Tigers did just that—their .340 OBP and 204 thefts both ranked third in the league, as did the team earned run average of a deep rotation with no ace. They won their first five and even hung around the pennant race until a six-game losing streak in late June from which they never recovered.

Fans who figured they would take their momentum and run with it were in for a rude awakening. Nearly every hitter who thrived the previous season collapsed in 1902, including infielders Dillon, Kid Gleason, and Kid Elberfeld and outfielder Ducky Holmes. The Tigers ranked dead last in runs scored, lost 35 of 44 games in the heat of the summer, and plummeted to seventh in the standings at 52-83.

They rebounded toward mediocrity over the next two seasons, but the most historically intriguing move during that time was the hiring of Ed Barrow as manager. The 34-year-old former mail clerk at an Iowa newspaper was born in a covered wagon to a pioneer family in the western territories. His passion for baseball led to successful talent

Ed Barrow gained far greater success as general manager of the Yankees than he did after taking the reins of the Tigers.
COURTESY OF THE NATIONAL BASEBALL HALL OF FAME LIBRARY

evaluation before he even reached the world of professional baseball. He discovered future Hall of Fame outfielder Fred Clarke among his newsboy staff as head of circulation. Barrow eventually earned enough money to purchase small baseball teams during the 1890s and serve as a field manager. Included among his achievements was recognizing the greatness of immortal shortstop Honus Wagner and signing him to his first professional contract.

Barrow was named president of the fledgling Atlantic League in 1897, then bought an Eastern League team in Toronto before taking over as Tigers manager in 1903. His tenure proved inconsequential. Detroit got off to what had become a typical fast start in his first year before fading to .500 and collapsing in late September. A terrible May the following season and disagreements with management motivated Barrow to resign after just a year-and-a-half at the helm.

He remained out of the spotlight until 1918, when he began in earnest his Hall of Fame career in baseball management. Barrow managed the Boston Red Sox to a World Series title that season while finally showing that somebody had the courage to transform Babe Ruth from pitcher to full-time starting outfielder. He then served as a centerpiece of the Yankees front office after the Sultan of Swat was sold to that team. Barrow became chief executive under owner Jacob Ruppert for a quarter century to help the Bronx Bombers blossom into the greatest dynasty in the history of American team sports.

Meanwhile, the Tigers continued to founder in 1905. They had lost 22 of 31 to fall nine games under .500 in late August when they purchased the contract of a feisty 18-year-old outfielder from Augusta of the South Atlantic League. He provided a spark that propelled his team to a 25-11 record down the stretch. His name was Ty Cobb. And he was about to lead a transformation of the pussycats into the beast of the American League.

CHAPTER THREE

Clawing Their Way to the Top

THE NOTION THAT TY COBB SINGLE-HANDEDLY TURNED THE TIGERS from tame kitties to monsters should be dismissed. The belief that he played the most significant role must be embraced.

It did not happen overnight. His immediate impact was muted over the death of his father, who was alleged to have been murdered by his mother for supposed infidelity. The court trial, as well as the brutal treatment he received as a 19-year-old newcomer early in the 1906 season, prevented Cobb from maximizing his potential and that of the Tigers. Cobb sizzled in September to finish with a team-high .315 batting average and lead his club to a nine-game winning streak. He proved his and his team's capabilities when performing their best. But they needed far more production from a weak lineup.

Cobb was one of only two players who could not be blamed for the Tigers ranking seventh in the American League in runs scored. The other was fellow outfielder and future Hall of Famer Sam Crawford. The triples machine who remains the all-time major-league leader in that department bolted the National League Cincinnati Reds for Detroit in 1903 and played the role of Robin to Cobb's Batman for more than a decade. Crawford led the league in triples six times and was considered a power hitter during the Dead Ball Era. He paced the American League with a "whopping" seven home runs in 1908 and in RBIs three times from 1910 to 1915 while also displaying tremendous speed as one of the premier base-stealers in franchise history.

But the Tigers could not win with two great hitters and decent pitching. Owner Bill Yawkey, who made a fortune in the mining and timber industry but gained more notoriety as uncle of legendary Red Sox owner Tom Yawkey, decided his team also needed a new manager. So he fired Bill Armour, who had been deemed too lenient with his players. Armour announced in mid-September that he would not return the following year. But he did not depart before being socked a few times under the grandstand by Washington catcher Jack Warner, who did not appreciate his treatment from Armour during his time with the Tigers.

Yawkey replaced him in 1907 with 38-year-old player-manager Hugh Jennings, whose cheerful nature and infectious optimism fired Cobb's enthusiasm and competitive spirit. Jennings's iconic "Ee-yah!" yell echoed around the ballpark—he even claimed to have placed the inspiring expression "attaboy" into the American lexicon.[1]

Hugh Jennings took over as manager in 1907 and remained at the helm for 13 years.
COURTESY OF THE LIBRARY OF CONGRESS

Jennings not only received far greater production from Cobb and Crawford but offensive help from flash-in-the-pan first baseman Claude Rossman and outfielder Davy Jones, who scored 101 runs in easily his finest season. Detroit skyrocketed from seventh in the American League in runs scored in 1906 to first while benefiting from a deep and talented rotation that included 20-game winners Ed Killian, George Mullin, and Bill Donovan, whose 25-4 record translated into the top winning percentage in franchise history until Max Scherzer won 21 of 24 decisions in 2013.

Not that the Tigers blew away the competition. They only managed to hang around the periphery of the pennant race behind the Athletics, who were managed by the legendary Connie Mack, and the sizzling Chicago White Sox. The Tigers fell 7½ games out of first place in mid-July when they caught fire. A 15-3 run that included a sweep of Philadelphia catapulted them into the lead. The rest of the season featured a nip-and-tuck battle with the Athletics as the Sox faded. The Tigers all but put away the pennant with a four-game blitz of pathetic Washington, then clinched it with a 10–2 defeat of St. Louis that featured a double and homer by Cobb.

Detroit baseball fans went crazy. They responded with giant bonfires, chanting and cheering throughout the city, and even painting their dogs with black tiger stripes. Observed one reporter, "One only had to stroll up and down one of the main streets yesterday to realize he was in 'Tigertown.' They are a very chesty lot—the inhabitants of the city where life is worth living—these days. They go about with expanded diaphragms and heads high in the air, for are not the Tigers winners of the American League and champion of the world and even of Mars as soon as they attend to the detail of disposing of the Chicago Cubs?"[2]

Talk about easier said than done! The powerful Cubs had played with a chip on their shoulders all year. They came in breathing fire after winning a then record 116 games in 1906 before blowing the World Series. They yearned to take their anger out on the Tigers and prove their historical greatness. Mission accomplished.

Perhaps it would not have been accomplished had the Tigers put away an opener in Chicago they appeared destined to win. Donovan took a 3–1 lead into the ninth inning. The Cubs scored a run with two outs, then pinch-hitter George Howard (who oddly was born and died on Christmas Eve) seemed to have fanned to end it when umpire Hank O'Day signaled a called strike three. O'Day had not noticed the ball scooting behind Detroit catcher Charlie Schmidt, a tough ex-boxer who was playing gamely with a fractured hand. The tying run scored and the game continued into the 12th inning when it was called due to darkness.

The Tigers never recovered from the blown opportunity. They scored only one run in each of the next three games and were blanked by Hall of Famer Mordecai "Three Finger" Brown in the clincher. They consistently failed to hit in the clutch—a 10-hit effort in Game 2 even resulted in just the single tally. Cobb batted just .200 in the series and failed to contribute an RBI.

Dampened spirits did not last long. The Tigers again joined the fray for the American League crown in 1908, greatly through the efforts of the outfield triumvirate of Cobb, Crawford, and Matty McIntyre, who came out of nowhere to bat .295 and pace the junior circuit with 105 runs scored. The addition of rookie right-hander Ed Summers, who compiled a 24-12 record and team-best 1.64 ERA, strengthened an already stout rotation.

Though one could argue that the 1967 AL pennant race was the most torrid of all time, the 1908 battle royal is certainly in the argument. The Tigers underachieved into late June to fall 4½ games behind, embarked on a 25-6 run to take a 3-game lead heading into August, then battled Cleveland and Chicago tooth-and-nail the rest of the way. Two early-October defeats in the Windy City placed them a mere half-game ahead of both rivals with one game remaining. They required a win over the White Sox to win the pennant. And they got it, courtesy of a two-hit shutout by Donovan, four hits from Crawford, and a ridiculous six Sox errors.

The Tigers were not done playing Chicago teams—a revenge match against the Cubs awaited. But their World Series foes proved again too powerful. Detroit finally broke out its bats in an 8–3 victory in Game 3 that featured four hits and two stolen bases by Cobb, but they went back into cold storage when the event returned to Bennett Park. The Tigers were blanked on just seven hits in Games 4 and 5 combined and left the field figuratively with their tails between their legs. One could not blame the down-to-the-wire pennant race for taking the steam out of the losers—the Cubs had also emerged from a massive struggle for the National League crown.

Sam Crawford played brilliantly in the shadow of Ty Cobb.
COURTESY OF THE LIBRARY OF CONGRESS

One significant factor in the Tigers' offensive problems in the Fall Classic was a lack of depth beyond Crawford and Cobb (whose only home-run title allowed him to win the Triple Crown that year). It reared its ugly head again in the regular season in 1909. The team again led the American League in scoring but were far too dependent on the two-headed monster, who combined for 204 RBIs. Nary a teammate drove in more than 39. The only other major contributor was second baseman Donie Bush, who led the league in walks (he would repeat that feat four more times) and tallied 115 runs.

That made it particularly difficult for the Tigers to string enough hits together in the Dead Ball Era to overcome superior pitching in the World Series. And they got there again in 1909 but not until fighting off more challenges. They seemed determined during the heat of the summer to win the pennant without a knock-out, drag-out fight, embarking on a franchise-record 14-game winning streak that remains the longest in franchise history (though tied in 1934) to stretch their lead to five games in early September. They continued to maintain what was considered a safe advantage until losing three of four in Philadelphia to allow the Athletics to close to within two games of first place.

Both the bats and arms came to life down the stretch to secure a third consecutive AL title. Also considered welcome news to some was that the Pirates and not the Cubs awaited the Tigers in the World Series. But Pittsburgh was a perennial contender that had won 106 regular-season games.

The clash featured an eagerly awaited battle between hunting buddies and personality polar opposites Cobb and Pirates slugger Honus Wagner, the two most dangerous hitters in the sport. And it was won by the latter, who not only outperformed Cobb but slammed a two-run triple in the first Game 7 in World Series history to propel his team to the crown. The Tigers star certainly understood that he had met his match. Cobb was not one to deliver unearned praise, but he once offered about Wagner, "That god damned Dutchman is the only man in the game I can't scare."[3]

Cobb was not the lone Tiger to blame for yet another ultimate defeat. The rotation triumvirate of George Mullin, Ed Willett, and Ed Summers, who combined for 69 victories in the regular season, lost all three of their decisions. Summers was knocked out in the first inning of Game 3, returned on one day's rest for Game 5, and was battered again.

Little could anyone have imagined that a world war would have been fought, Prohibition come and gone, Cobb long retired, and America in the midst of a devastating depression before the Tigers returned to the Fall Classic. Jennings continued to guide his team to winning seasons into the second decade of the 20th century, but the dominance of Connie Mack and his Athletics precluded any run to contention. Detroit remained one of the premier offensive clubs in the American League, but its pitching staff deteriorated. Its team ERA dropped from third-last in 1910 to second-last in 1911 and 1912 to dead last in 1913. By that time only a fading Willett remained among those that pitched the Tigers to three straight pennants.

Players came and went. One who did hang around for more than a decade beyond was Cobb, perhaps the most colorful, hated, and some contend misunderstood player in baseball history.

CHAPTER FOUR

The Georgia Peach

THE SANDS OF TIME CAN EITHER CLARIFY OR BLUR THE REALITIES OF the distant past. One example is Ty Cobb. That he is arguably the greatest hitter in baseball history is clear. His statistics scream out that truth. Yet Cobb is also arguably the most reviled ballplayer ever (though suspected steroid abuser and all-time home-run champ Barry Bonds has certainly sidled up close in the rankings). It has been written that Cobb was a racist. It has been claimed he intentionally sought to injure fielders on the basepaths. It has been stated that he was an illiterate with no desire to educate himself. But other research has asserted that it has revealed the opposite. It has contested that Cobb was an intelligent and friendly man who was simply driven by a passion for baseball and winning.

The legendary and feared Ty Cobb (right and sliding middle)
COURTESY OF THE LIBRARY OF CONGRESS

Perhaps the truth lies somewhere in between. Whatever the reality, what cannot be debated is that Cobb experienced tragedy that certainly complicated his legacy. His life began on December 18, 1886, in The Narrows, Georgia. The son of a schoolteacher father and mother from a well-to-do family, Ty and his brother Paul, who toiled nine years as a minor leaguer trying in vain to reach the big leagues, spent endless hours as kids playing baseball. His highly educated dad preferred that he concentrate more on his studies, but that wish was rejected. Cobb preferred honing his skills on the diamond to book learning. So much for his parents' dream of a career as a lawyer or doctor. Yet despite the push back the boy grew to idolize his father, offering years later that he was "the greatest man I ever knew . . . I worshiped him."[1]

The man he worshiped continued to push back against his career aspirations despite his obvious and burgeoning talents. The young Cobb emerged as a standout for a local adult team after landing a roster spot at the tender age of 14. Dad not only finally relented when his son began pursuing a baseball career—he encouraged him. Though he first tried to talk Ty out of a spring training invite from the Augusta Tourists of the South Atlantic League, he gave him a pep talk once he realized the discouragement was fruitless. His father told him to give baseball everything he had.

That would not be a problem. Cobb played the sport with passion and abandon. Though his tryout with Augusta failed, he soon landed with a semipro club in Anniston, Alabama. His dad warned him to not return a failure, an admonition that proved inspiring. He performed so well that he was given another opportunity with Augusta that included an invitation to spring training and two exhibition games against the Tigers, who came away impressed with his skills, aggressiveness, and enthusiasm for the sport.

Cobb struggled at the plate during the regular season with Augusta until new manager George Leidy came to the rescue. He encouraged Cobb to maximize his talent by teaching him the nuances of the game. Coupled with his natural intensity, the 18-year-old used that knowledge to blossom into the premier hitter in the South Atlantic League. Soon the Tigers and their rivals began eyeing him as a potentially impactful talent.

Detroit purchased the contract of the 18-year-old for $700 and summoned him for a cup of coffee on August 30, 1905. But not before he experienced a tragedy that took the man he worshipped out of his life. The intrigue began when his father left the house on an August evening and informed wife Amanda that he would not be returning until the following day. Driven by suspicion that she was having an affair, he procured a pistol and returned home. A confrontation allegedly ensued in which Amanda fired two bullets into her husband and killed him.

She claimed to have mistaken him for a burglar and was cleared of manslaughter charges in 1906, but what mattered to the teenager trying to forge a baseball career was that his beloved father was gone. His loss affected Cobb both personally and professionally. He lived his life and played the game angrily as if seeking to avenge the death of his dad on anyone he perceived to be in his way. Asked why he made so many enemies during his baseball career, he responded, "I did it for my father. . . . I knew he was watching me and I never let him down."[2]

If Dad were indeed peeking from the great beyond, he would not have been disappointed in his son. The grieving Cobb could not have been blamed for allowing the tragedy to affect his play on the field. But the wild abandon with which he performed before the murder of his father gained intensity. And so did his refusal to deal with any perceived slight rationally and peacefully. He reacted with resentment to the typical rookie hazing from teammates, whose actions inspired his wrath for many years. While he grieved as his mother stood trial during 1906 spring training, his thoughtless fellow Tigers humiliated him by ruining his ballcaps and bats. Cobb was not one to forgive and forget.

But just how vengeful and hateful Cobb became is a matter of debate, as is the charge of racism. Negro League standout pitcher Ted Radcliffe, who faced Cobb in an exhibition in Cuba, claimed in a 1997 interview that "Ty Cobb was a racist. I threw him out three times and he quit. He said, 'No nigger gonna throw me out.'"

Biographies and magazine articles before and after Radcliffe made that assertion sought to confirm his view. So did a generally accepted incident that occurred in 1907 when Cobb violently attacked a Black groundskeeper whose greeting he perceived as disrespectful, then choked his wife nearly to death when she attempted to intervene, stopping only when a teammate knocked him cold. A year later he attacked a Black worker when he complained that Cobb had walked through freshly poured asphalt. That incident resulted in a charge of assault and battery. In 1909 a Black night watchman accused Cobb of attempted murder after he had been beaten in Cleveland. Cobb pled guilty to a lesser charge and the suit was settled out of court.

Some assume Cobb was a racist because he was born and raised in the South before the turn of the 20th century. Jim Crowism had been firmly established, lynching was common, and the destruction of Reconstruction had resulted not only in rampant discrimination but also a widespread belief in Black inferiority.

But biographer Charles Leerhsen offered quite a different opinion after researching the life and times of the man nicknamed The Georgia Peach. The author learned that Cobb's descendants were abolitionists before the Civil War. Among them was his great-grandfather, a preacher who railed against slavery and refused to fight for the Confederacy. During a stint as a state senator, Cobb's father broke up a lynch mob and was voted out of office because of it. Cobb himself spoke about the right of Blacks to play in the major leagues in 1952, five years after Jackie Robinson had integrated the sport.

Leerhsen claimed that a biography written by Al Stump in the 1990s resulted in false quotes and concocted incidents. Perhaps, however, the conflicting viewpoints were the consequence of Cobb changing and softening over the years. What the angry young ballplayer said and did around the second decade of the 20th century might have differed from what he felt and believed 40 years later.

What remains undisputed is that though the rejection of education in the classroom prevented Cobb from being book smart, his baseball savvy made him one of the most intelligent players in the game. He embraced every edge he could find, especially at the plate and on the basepaths. He studied each pitcher to learn their weaknesses. He ran aggressively, even stealing and taking extra bases in lopsided games to plant fear in the hearts and minds of opponents he believed might cause critical errors during closer contests.

Cobb quickly emerged as the biggest star in the sport despite his unpopularity among teammates and foes. He was so competitive that he sat out the final two games of the 1910 season to ensure a batting crown ahead of Cleveland hitting machine Nap Lajoie, who was seven points behind and seemingly had no chance to catch him. But St. Louis Browns manager Jack "Peach Pie" O'Connor, one of many in baseball who despised Cobb, hatched a plan. He ordered his third baseman to play in shallow left field, allowing Lajoie to dribble seven bunt singles down the line, conclude the doubleheader with eight hits, and forge ahead for the batting title. Cobb got the last laugh, however, when further research showed that his statistics for one game were counted twice and that he actually finished one point ahead of Lajoie. He is still recognized by the sport as the 1910 batting champion.

More controversy followed in 1912 when Cobb raced into the stands during a road game against the New York Highlanders to punch and stomp on with his cleats a heckler who had lost one hand and three fingers on his other in a manufacturing accident. When fans screamed for him to stop punching someone who could certainly not defend himself, Cobb replied, "I don't care if he has no feet."[3] Though the attack was not defendable, critics of the angry superstar did not know that the man he had battered relentlessly heckled Cobb from what he believed to be the safe haven of the stands every time the Tigers visited. The Detroit players, who had urged Cobb to attack and even held back fans who tried to help the hapless victim, went on strike when their teammate was suspended indefinitely after the incident. That forced baseball commissioner Ban Johnson to reduce the suspension to 10 games.

Cobb, who felt strongly principled at least in his own mind, refused to accept what he considered disrespect from anyone, even Tigers owner Frank Navin. After winning his sixth consecutive batting title in 1912, hitting over .400 over the previous two seasons, winning Most Valuable Player honors in 1911, and leading the league in RBIs in four of the last five years, Cobb staged a highly publicized holdout. He demanded a significant raise after earning nine grand every year from 1910 to 1912. Cobb understood that the franchise was raking in the bucks as fans had been flocking to new Navin Field. He knew all about the growing population of Detroit during the growth of the automobile industry, felt rightly that patrons were greatly motivated to watch him perform, and wanted a bigger piece of the pie. So he asked for $15,000 and stated emphatically that he would not report to 1913 spring training unless he got it. Never mind the Reserve Clause of that era and beyond that tied players to their teams in perpetuity.

Navin battled back in the press. "Cobb will not get what he is demanding," he exclaimed. "He will get no $15,000 a year, and if he refuses to sign a contract at what we consider a fair figure we will get along without him, as we have done before. I intend to run the Detroit Base Ball Club for a while yet. If Cobb buys it, then he can run it to suit himself, but as long as I am at its head I shall manage it as I believe best. . . . It won't break my heart if he [doesn't sign]."[4]

Cobb issued the following retort in a press release from his Georgia home: "I have only asked for what I believe that I am worth, and it certainly does seem that a man should be able to do that without drawing such a statement from the club president as Mr. Navin is reported to have made. He certainly does not own me, body and soul."[5]

The result of the public wrangling and negotiation was a far less significant salary increase to $12,000 that was lessened to $11,333 to account for time absent. Cobb did not miss a beat upon his return. He hit safely in 20 of 22 games during one early-season stretch as his batting average peaked in late May to a ridiculous .508. He won six more batting titles following the holdout, managed his last .400 season in 1922, and finished his career as a 12-time batting champion who led the league in hits eight times, on-base percentage seven times, and stolen bases six times. He finished his career as the all-time leader in thefts with 897, a modern-day mark that remained unbroken until shattered a half-century later by Lou Brock. Cobb's .366 lifetime batting average might never be overcome.

That even four of 226 voters refused to place him on their Hall of Fame ballots in 1936 was either a testament to stupidity or Cobb's combative nature. The former reason is more likely—even Babe Ruth and Willie Mays did not receive 100 percent approval for the Hall.

Tigers owner Frank Navin battled Ty Cobb over big bucks at the bargaining table.
COURTESY OF THE NATIONAL BASEBALL HALL OF FAME LIBRARY

A lack of talent beyond Cobb, particularly after Sam Crawford retired following the 1917 season, prevented the Tigers from winning another pennant until 1934. They bounced from mediocre to terrible in the late 1910s, leading the increasingly unpopular skipper Hugh Jennings to resign by mutual consent with Navin, who convinced a reluctant Cobb to serve as player-manager, a role that some worried did not suit him. Cobb had by that time gained interests beyond baseball that increased his wealth, including investments into such burgeoning companies as United Motors (which merged with General Motors in 1918) and Coca-Cola. He remained at the helm from 1921 to 1926 with mixed success that included four consecutive winning seasons. He guided the 1924 Tigers into a pennant race, but they faded away by mid-September.

Cobb would certainly not be remembered for his stint as manager, though his mentoring of younger talent such as Harry Heilmann proved beneficial to future franchise fortunes. His legacy remains as arguably the most dangerous hitter and feistiest player to ever don a major-league uniform. His character has been the subject of debate for generations—a gambling scandal forced him out of Detroit in 1927. But what few can argue is that Ty Cobb was the greatest Tiger of all time.

CHAPTER FIVE

The Yo-Yo Years

GAMBLING WAS BIG BUSINESS IN BASEBALL BEFORE NEW COMMISSIONER Kenesaw Mountain Landis cleaned up the sport following the Black Sox scandal of 1919 and 1920. But anyone who bet on the Tigers during that era based on their performance the previous season lost their shirts. They failed when they were expected to succeed and succeeded when they were expected to fail.

Those that anticipated disaster in 1915 after two losing campaigns and a mediocre one were in for a shock. That Ty Cobb and Sam Crawford continued to hit came as no surprise. But that fellow outfielder Bobby Veach would begin his ascent to greatness with one of the finest seasons in franchise history certainly did. The easygoing Kentuckian from a coal mining family belied his 160-pound frame by hitting for power. He led the American League with 40 doubles and 112 runs batted in that year, launching a productive career that concluded with a .310 batting average, four RBI titles, and borderline Hall of Fame credentials. His emergence helped the 1915 Tigers tally 163 more times than they had the previous season and rank first in the league in runs scored.

The beneficiaries were rotation stalwarts Hooks Dauss, Jean Dubuc, and Harry Coveleski, whose brother and fellow pitcher Stan soon launched a brilliant career with the Indians. All three performed better than they had in 1914 as the Tigers embarked on a run to contention. They wasted little time vaulting into the lead with an eight-game winning streak in April and bolting to an 18-7 record. They faded to the periphery of the race in late June before rebounding and remaining

Bobby Veach put together a sensational season in 1915.
COURTESY OF THE LIBRARY OF CONGRESS

neck-and-neck with the Red Sox, who were thriving behind new pitching sensation Babe Ruth. A 16-3 blitz to open August that peaked with a nine-game winning streak catapulted Detroit to the top. A four-game series at Fenway Park in mid-September that attracted over 100,000 fans was destined to determine the champion.

It did not go well for the Tigers after a balanced batting attack and fine performance by Dauss resulted in a 6–1 victory in the opener and pushed them to within one game of the lead. They scored just four runs over the last three games, wasting a brilliant effort by Coveleski in the process. He pitched into the 12th inning of a 1–0 defeat. The series loss sent the Tigers four games behind. They finished hot for their first 100-win season but could not recover. The Sox took their momentum and ran with it to a World Series championship.

That Detroit could take its momentum to a crown in 1916 did not seem far-fetched. But the yo-yo swings of its clubs of that era had been established. Those that believed they knew what to expect were fooling themselves. More than 600,000 fans streamed into Navin Field that year to place the Tigers second in American League attendance, but the team could not match its dominance of the previous season. The main culprits were Crawford, whose collapse came suddenly and would end his career a year later, and the starting pitchers aside from Coveleski and Dauss. The lack of rotation depth resulted in the Tigers dropping to a lowly seventh in the American League in team ERA.

Not that they completely collapsed. They rebounded from an eight-game losing streak in May that dropped them to second-last in the standings with a 19-4 blitz that pushed them into a tie for first place. Another losing skein sent them reeling again, but they caught fire in late August to make a run for the pennant in what emerged as a more balanced race that also featured the Red Sox and White Sox. The Tigers won 14 of 17 to take over the lead but once again could not beat Boston, this time before comparatively big crowds at Navin Field. A three-game sweep that concluded with Ruth besting Coveleski, who was knocked out in the third inning, doomed Detroit to a third-place finish.

A generation passed before the Tigers strongly contended again. The immediate problem proved to be the demise of the pitching staff. A tired arm caused Coveleski to be shut down after early struggles in 1917 from which he never recovered. Soon the club sported the worst rotation in the American League. The Tigers trotted out a mish-mosh of starters, none of whom beyond Dauss proved particularly effective. The slugging triumvirate of Cobb, Heilmann, and Veach assured decent production but not winning ballclubs. Detroit dropped to 61-93 in 1920, signaling the end of the 14-year run of Hugh Jennings as manager. Cobb fared little better in his first season in charge as one-time Red Sox ace Dutch Leonard, who had been purchased in 1919, could not save a poor rotation in his descent to mediocrity.

An intriguing statistical reality during the Cobb tenure was that the Tigers did not require a dramatic increase in home runs to remain prolific offensively. Babe Ruth had destroyed the Dead Ball Era nearly single-handedly, and the Yankees led the league in longballs year after year. And rivals also began blasting balls over fences with far greater frequency. The Tigers were not among them. They finished close to the bottom of the American League in home runs consistently in the early 1920s yet ranked in the top three in runs scored every year from 1922 to 1926, including first in 1924 and 1925. Only Heilmann emerged as a consistent double-figure home-run threat during that period.

The Tigers dominated offensively the old-fashioned way—working counts to generate a high on-base percentage while utilizing their speed to steal bases and rack up doubles and triples. New standouts such as Hall of Fame outfielder Heinie Manush, catcher Johnny Bassler, and first baseman Lu Blue joined Cobb and Heilmann to create an offensive juggernaut. But the revolving-door rotation produced only one or two effective pitchers every season. The Tigers ranked in the bottom half of the league in team ERA four times between 1922 and 1926. Most of their starters sported earned run averages over 4.00. The desperate search for an ace failed.

Soon there would be a desperate search for a new manager. It was November 3, 1926, when the bombshell hit. Cobb announced he was not only resigning but retiring as a player as well. Many an eyebrow was raised when Cleveland manager and superstar outfielder Tris Speaker did the same on that very day. That proved three weeks later to be no coincidence when former Tigers pitcher Dutch Leonard sold letters to American League president Ban Johnson written by Cobb and Indians star pitcher Smoky Joe Wood proving that all four players had conspired to fix a game between the two teams on September 25, 1919. Cobb later admitted being among the four players involved but refused to acknowledge that he placed a $2,000 bet on the game, though strong evidence suggested he did.

Accusations of fixes were commonplace before the Black Sox scandal, and this one was of little consequence beyond the moral implications. The White Sox and Indians had already locked up the top two spots in the standings on the date the deed was done. For whatever reason, however, the Indians wanted the Tigers to finish ahead of the Yankees for third place, which garnered an estimated payment of $500 per player. So they supposedly threw the game, which Detroit won, 9–5. The outcome did not have the desired effect—New York still finished ahead of the Tigers.

And one could certainly claim Speaker did not work his tail off trying to blow it. He slammed two triples and a single in the defeat.

According to Leonard, he met with Cobb, Speaker, and Wood under the grandstand before the previous game and let the two Tigers know that they "didn't have to worry about tomorrow's game."[1] The group concluded that since the outcome had been decided they might as well throw down some bets that would be placed by ballpark attendant Fred West. The sudden increase in money being tossed around for that game scared away some bookmakers, resulting in only $600 bet among the four participants.

Cobb expressed regret two years later in a letter he wrote to Leonard. Wood claimed that Cobb did not make a cent on the fix. Meanwhile, Leonard followed through with a vendetta against Cobb, whom he disliked intensely. Leonard had been traded to a minor-league club in 1925 to which he refused to report, and he blamed the trade on Cobb. Leonard was also angry with Speaker for not picking him up to play for the Indians. That is why he released the letter to Johnson that implicated one and all. Leonard had nothing to lose—he had already been forced to retire. He threatened to sell the letters between Cobb and Wood to a Detroit newspaper. Johnson yearned to avoid another black eye for the sport and Tigers owner Frank Navin for his team. They decided to buy off Leonard rather than allow the scandal to reach the public. So they paid him $20,000, the amount he claimed the Tigers owed him for supposedly shortening his career.

That could not save Cobb. Johnson convinced him and Speaker to resign from their managerial positions and retire from the game. A skeptical Landis, who distrusted Johnson, decided to launch his own inquiry. Leonard refused to cooperate. Meanwhile, Cobb, Speaker, and Wood claimed their innocence and demanded an audience with Leonard, who declined the invitation to a verbal showdown.

Word soon leaked out about the scandal. The public firmly stood against Leonard, whom they deemed a vengeful sourpuss. Even veteran umpire Billy Evans, who engaged in a fistfight with Cobb under the grandstand six years earlier, sided with his former combatant. "Only a miserable thirst for vengeance actuated Leonard's attack on Cobb and

Speaker," Evans said. "It is a crime that men of the stature of Ty and Tris should be blackened by a man of this caliber with charges that every baseballer knows to be utterly false."[2]

Innocent or not, Cobb was through with the Tigers. But unlike Shoeless Joe Jackson and Pete Rose, whose gambling on baseball gained greater notoriety and has for decades kept them out of the Hall of Fame, his bust as well as that of Speaker remain in Cooperstown. And the Ban Johnson ban did not stick. Cobb signed with the Philadelphia Athletics and helped legendary manager Connie Mack and his crew remain an American League powerhouse for two more years.

His departure resulted in little change for the Tigers, who continued to bounce up and down the standings. Navin surprised the baseball community by replacing Cobb with former Detroit third baseman George Moriarty, who had since retiring as a player gained greater notoriety as an umpire. Like his predecessor at the helm Moriarty boasted a fiery personality. It was claimed that he once even intimidated Cobb out of a fight by handing him a bat and claiming he would need it. The bizarre choice as new skipper appeared justified in 1927 as the Tigers parlayed a 49-22 midseason stretch and strong finish into an 82-71 record.

Among the most encouraging performers was 24-year-old second baseman and future Hall of Famer Charlie Gehringer, who batted .317 and would soon emerge as both a stolen base and home-run threat. The Tigers also benefited from the finest season for popular outfielder Bob Fothergill, who was known in Detroit as "The People's Choice." He took advantage of Cobb's departure and additional playing time by batting .359 and driving in a career-high 114 runs. But, alas, he never again served as a full-time starter despite his production and faded in his early 30s.

Moriarty was not long for the Tigers bench, though one could not blame a woeful lack of pitching on him. His club featured enough power, speed, and pure hitting to remain among the more potent offensive clubs in the American League in 1928. But only a strong season from flash-in-the-pan journeyman Ownie Carroll prevented total disaster from the pitching staff that year. The Tigers finished 68-86, their worst record since 1920, and soon thereafter Moriarty was back behind the catcher calling balls and strikes.

**Charlie Gehringer really took off in 1927 and emerged
as a Hall of Famer.**
COURTESY OF THE NATIONAL BASEBALL HALL OF FAME LIBRARY

Among the mistakes made by the organization before that year was trading Manush to the St. Louis Browns. The Hall of Fame outfielder had struggled—at least to his standards—upon the departure of Cobb. Not only had his batting average dropped 80 points to .298 in 1927, but he did not get along with Moriarty. The new manager forced the deal that sent away Manush and Blue for the nondescript duo of Harry Rice, who gave them two strong years before struggling, and all-but-cooked pitcher Elam Vangilder. Manush led the American League in hits with 241 in his first year with St. Louis and matched his .378 average from 1925, then continued to hit with the Browns and Senators for more than a decade.

Inheriting the mess in 1929 was Bucky Harris, who had managed Walter Johnson and the Washington Senators to the World Series title in 1924 and another American League pennant the following year. But there was no "Big Train" in the Detroit rotation, which instead careened off the rails. The Tigers bizarrely boasted five .300 hitters in their starting lineup, led the AL in runs scored, and nearly doubled their attendance from the previous season, yet finished 70-84. Nary a starter compiled an ERA under 4.08 as Carroll collapsed and the rotation descended to the worst in the sport aside from the pathetic Phillies. Navin had simply not provided Harris with the horses to compete. And when the young pitchers rebounded to at least mediocrity in the early 1930s, the offense dropped to the same level.

Among the everyday players who fell from grace was Dale Alexander. The first baseman slammed pitches with such authority for Toronto in the International League, even winning the Triple Crown in that circuit in 1928, that the *Atlanta Constitution* raved that "he can hit a ball almost as hard as Babe Ruth" and compared him to Hall of Fame slugger Sam Crawford.[3] Alexander exploded onto the scene by batting .343 and leading the American League in hits with 215 while driving in 137 as a rookie in 1929. The first rookie to amass more than 200 hits since Shoeless Joe Jackson in 1911 then added 20 home runs and 135 RBIs in 1930. Alexander lost his power stroke the next season but slammed 47 doubles. The problem was his defense. He committed a whopping 56 errors over his first three seasons at first base and was placed on waivers in 1932. Alexander landed in Boston, where he won the batting title that year before losing his magic at the plate.

By that time another of the all-time Tiger greats had joined Cobb among the ranks of retirees. And that was Harry Heilmann. But the man who had lived in Cobb's shadow certainly did not deserve his destiny as second fiddle during the peak of his incredible career.

CHAPTER SIX

Just Wild about Harry

THE SHADOW CAST BY TY COBB WAS LONG AND DARK. IT TENDED TO envelop anyone in its wake. His greatness as a hitter and strength of personality left little room for teammates to make a mark. In the grand scheme of baseball history, nobody who played alongside Cobb could possibly earn the notoriety he deserved.

Welcome to the world of Harry Heilmann, one of the most underappreciated, even unrecognized players to ever don a major-league uniform. He did not slide into bases spikes high. He did not engage in fistfights. He did not verbally attack fellow players. He just went about his business with cool efficiency and devastated opponents. Heilmann reached double figures in doubles, triples, and home runs in six different seasons during his Hall of Fame career. He would still be the last American League player to bat over .400 had Ted Williams not achieved that feat in 1941. And he even stole 113 bases with savvy and smarts—he could not run a lick.

The son of second-generation Irish parents, Heilmann was born in San Francisco on August 3, 1894. His father, who ran a soap manufacturing business, died at age 36. That was not the only tragedy the boy suffered in his young life. He watched as more than 3,000 residents were killed by the devastating earthquake that rocked the city in 1906, then lost his brother Walter two years later to a boating accident.

Baseball had grown quite popular in the Bay Area despite the fact that no major-league team played west of St. Louis until the New York Giants moved to San Francisco in 1958. But Heilmann, strangely

Harry Heilmann could do it all on a baseball diamond.
COURTESY OF THE LIBRARY OF CONGRESS

considering his career arc, did not play the sport while attending Sacred Heart High School (though he performed well in pickup games). It has been offered that he first eschewed the sport so that he would not be compared unfavorably to Walter, a pitcher with a fine curveball and control who was considered the future baseball star in the family, then refused to play after his brother lost his life. Other reports have conflicted on whether Harry was cut from the baseball team or simply opted not to try out. He certainly remained active at the prep level competing in football, track, and basketball, earning all-state honors in the latter.

The image of Heilmann as a quiet, unassuming type—quite the contrast to Cobb—is furthered by his work as a bookkeeper for the Mutual Biscuit Company at age 19. Fate soon stepped in. A former high school classmate asked Heilmann to replace him for a semipro game in nearby Hanford, which it is believed competed in the San Joaquin Valley League.

The task that promised him what was then a not-so-measly 10 bucks resulted in far more than a little exercise and some quick cash. It changed his life. Heilmann slugged a game-winning double in the 11th inning and had piqued the interest of a Northwest League scout, who Heilmann later recalled lured him to play for the Portland Beavers by taking him out for a spaghetti dinner that served as a signing bonus. The Northwest League was the dregs of minor-league baseball, but it was a start for Heilmann. The Beavers were the farm team of a namesake club in the Pacific Coast League, which featured the premier players on the West Coast.

He wasted little time showing off the talent that had been obscured by what one might assume based on his abilities was a decision not to play high school baseball. After a sorry start to his professional career in which he went hitless in three at-bats and committed an error at first base, he began to make his mark. Heilmann batted over .300 to motivate Northwest League president Fielder Jones to recommend him to Tigers owner Frank Navin, who signed him to a contract reported to be around $1,000.

His potential seemed pronounced during spring training in 1914, but the 19-year-old performed horribly to start that season, particularly in the outfield. He earned the nickname "slug" for the snail's pace in which he tracked balls. In one particularly disturbing exhibition, he showed negative versatility in committing three errors—one by fumbling a single into a double, another by overthrowing second base, and yet another by dropping a flyball. It was no wonder the Tigers tried in vain after his mid-May arrival to transform him into an infielder.

Merely months after toiling away as a bookkeeper Heilmann was serving as a jack-of-all-trades for Detroit. He played outfield, first base, and second base after his mid-May arrival. And though he batted a mere .225 for the Tigers that season and was shipped to the minor-league San Francisco Seals in 1915 for more seasoning, his promise was undeniable. He was deemed the heir apparent to triples machine Sam Crawford, who had decided to remain active for a bit longer.

Crawford hung around in 1916, but the Tigers could not wait to utilize Heilmann's vast talents. Manager Hughie Jennings placed him all over the diamond to get his bat into the lineup. And though the Dead Ball Era played a role in preventing Heilmann from exhibiting the power he would eventually spotlight, he proved quite productive from the start, batting .282 with 77 RBIs in his first full season.

That breakthrough could not compare to the valor he displayed off the field on July 25. Late that evening, while driving, he spotted a vehicle back off a dock and fall into the Detroit River. So he jumped from his car and into the water to save three of the five passengers. The media trumpeted Heilmann as a hero, but one can imagine that the incident, which cost the lives of a mother and daughter, brought stark memories of how his brother died. An emotional tribute to Heilmann the next day at Navin Field inspired a standing ovation.

By the following year he had emerged as a full-time outfielder, though the Tigers continued to use him occasionally at first base throughout his career. But he did not blossom into a premier hitter until raising his average to .320 in 1919 after spending half the previous season serving on a submarine in World War I.

One might assume wearing the same uniform as Ty Cobb would have benefited Heilmann at the plate immediately. After all, who better to advise the kid on maximizing his hitting potential? But though Cobb claimed later to have detected several flaws in the batting stance of his teammate, he chose not to bring them to the attention of Heilmann until landing the managerial job in 1921. Cobb admitted that he did not feel comfortable giving advice to his peer but considered it his job once he took over the helm.

The results proved stunning. Heilmann smoked opposing American League pitchers in 1921 for a .394 batting average after hitting a fine-but-unspectacular .309 in 1920. So lethal had Heilmann become that he maintained a .500 batting average into mid-May and remained over .400 until fading in late September (his year-end mark was his lowest of the season). Heilmann stayed ahead of Cobb throughout the year for the American League batting title, which it has been claimed damaged the ego of his proud manager, who refused thereafter to communicate with his budding star off the field.

Heilmann even fell victim early in his career to Cobb's penchant for platooning. Cobb also created a split between Heilmann and Bobby Veach, the third stud in the super outfield. Cobb believed Veach did not play the game with what he perceived as requisite passion, so he pushed Heilmann to push Veach—at least verbally. The motivation was that the easygoing Veach would respond by hustling more, never mind that he had already thrice led the league in RBIs and in 1919 paced one and all in hits, doubles, and triples. Veach did manage his finest seasons with Heilmann riding him in 1921 and 1922, but Cobb never revealed to him that he had demanded that his teammate drive him. The result was a strained relationship between Heilmann and Veach until the latter was waived before the 1924 season.

By that time Heilmann had established a pattern of exceeding or approaching a .400 average on odd years and performing merely brilliantly in the even ones. He led the American League in hitting in 1921, 1923, 1925, and 1927, beating out in each of those years the still-dangerous Cobb, who failed to win a batting crown after 1919.

After fading in the waning days of the 1921 season to fall under .400, Heilmann did the opposite to reach the coveted goal two years later. His quest appeared doomed when his average fell to .387 after managing just one hit in a September 20 doubleheader in Boston. But he swung his bat like a magic wand thereafter, slamming 26 hits in 47 at-bats for a ridiculous .551 mark to finish the year at .403. Heilmann hit at least .393 in the other three seasons in which he captured batting titles. A few more hits here and there and he would have been the only player in major-league history to reach .400 four times. He joked that since he was playing under a series of two-year contracts he would be motivated only in the odd years to perform his best. Not that he struggled otherwise—he batted at least .346 in the even years sandwiched between.

So popular had he become in Detroit that 40,000 fans showed up to Harry Heilmann Day, which was held at Navin Field on August 9, 1926. Among the gifts received by the man who had earned the nickname Harry the Horse were a new car, diamond stickpin, and hunting dog. He was certainly forgiven for going hitless that afternoon in a loss to the Yankees.

His 1927 batting title required a torrid finish. He had captured the crown in each of the previous three odd years, but young Athletics outfielder and future Hall of Famer Al Simmons led Heilmann by one point heading into the final day of the season. Normally the two-hit performance by Simmons that afternoon would have precluded a leapfrog by Heilmann, but the latter smashed seven hits against Cleveland in a doubleheader to skyrocket his average to .398. He could have called it a season after his third hit in the opener. Fans screamed out that he had Simmons beaten. But Heilmann refused and clobbered a home run in his next at-bat. He received a standing ovation as he took the field for Game 2, then fell just a triple short of hitting for the cycle in that one.

That Heilmann could ever lead the league in hitting speaks of his ability to make consistently hard contact. He certainly could not beat out many infield hits with his speed—or lack thereof. "Heilmann was never much faster than an ice wagon on the basepaths," offered New York sportswriter Tommy Holmes. "Without a doubt, he is the slowest moving great hitter who ever lived."[1]

The career arc of Heilmann matched trends in the sport. Heilmann began to blast more home runs after Babe Ruth ushered in the Live Ball Era, though he never emerged as a prodigious slugger. He averaged 15 home runs over his last 10 seasons (including with Cincinnati in 1930), a power surge that allowed him to grow into a prolific run producer. Heilmann exceeded 100 runs batted in every year but one from 1921 to 1929 and led the league with 134 in 1925. The only shame of it all is that Heilmann never gained the opportunity to show off his talents in a World Series.

He did, however, in another profession. He took public speaking classes and became the second player behind former Indians outfielder Jack Graney to serve as a radio announcer for the team with which he played. The Tigers asked waivers on Heilmann after he had batted "only" .344 in 1929 to finish eighth in the batting race. He ended his career with Cincinnati in 1932 after sitting out the previous year with arthritis. Heilmann returned to join the beloved Ty Tyson in the broadcast booth.

Describing the action from a ticker as announcers were forced to do for away games in that era proved quite a challenge, but Heilmann made the transition from ballplayer seamlessly. No less than immortal play-by-play man Red Barber, who did not utter praise easily, lauded Heilmann for his performance and work ethic. By 1943 his voice could be heard throughout a network of Michigan radio stations describing the exploits of such Detroit stars as Hank Greenberg, Charlie Gehringer, and Hal Newhouser.

Heilmann appeared destined to call Tigers games for decades to come but was diagnosed with lung cancer during spring training in 1951. He received that summer a visit in the hospital from Cobb, who told him falsely to bring him a sense of joy and fulfillment in his dying days that he had been elected to the Baseball Hall of Fame. Heilmann died on July 9 and was voted in posthumously a year later.

Many consider it a travesty that he was not chosen on the first ballot. Playing in the shadow of Cobb certainly weakened his legacy. But one cannot objectively study the career of Harry Heilmann and dispute that he should have been given the opportunity to walk through those hallowed halls in Cooperstown as a Hall of Famer.

CHAPTER SEVEN

One Pilfer, Two Pennants

THE TIGERS HAD BOTTOMED OUT. THEIR 61-93 MARK IN 1931 PUNCTU-
ated by a 3-22 collapse from mid-May to mid-June was their worst since
1902. The Harris era ended after two mediocre years followed. The Great
Depression had taken hold, Detroiters like all Americans prioritized
staying afloat financially over spending money on ballgames, and attendance at Navin Field tumbled. But in the midst of the national calamity
a Tigers team was about to stun the baseball world and lure fans back to
the ballpark.

It is not true that Tigers owner Frank Navin wore a mask and held a
gun to the head of Connie Mack at any point on December 12, 1933. His
venerable Philadelphia Athletics counterpart had been as the financial
times worsened selling off many of the players who had helped create a
dynasty, and Navin was quite happy to take advantage. He robbed Mack
of Hall of Fame catcher Mickey Cochrane, surrendering throwaway
backstop Johnny Pasek and $100,000. It was quite the early Christmas
present for Detroit fans.

Cochrane was acquired to do more than squat behind the plate and
maintain his status as a high-average doubles machine who annually
reached base at better than a .400 clip. He was brought in to manage
what had become a franchise wallowing in mediocrity. Such was not the
original intent of Navin, who wanted Bucky Harris to remain at the helm
despite those struggles. The owner tried to talk Harris out of quitting, but
the latter stated selflessly to the media that the Tigers could do better
than him.

Catcher Mickey Cochrane (right) played with great passion.
COURTESY OF THE NATIONAL BASEBALL HALL OF FAME LIBRARY

That turned out to be an understatement. The club went from mediocre to dynamite in its first season under Cochrane. Detroit exploded offensively with virtually the same lineup, though Cochrane certainly proved an upgrade over 1933 starting catcher Ray Hayworth with the bat, and the addition of veteran outfielder Goose Goslin played a significant role as well. Goslin had starred with St. Louis and Washington, but some considered him cooked at age 33 after his average sank to .297. That drop and his anger over being bypassed for the Senators' managerial position in favor of Joe Cronin resulted in a trade to Detroit for fellow outfielder John "Rocky" Stone. Goslin reverted to form in 1934, batting .305 with 100 RBIs and scoring 106 runs as one of five Tigers to reach triple figures in that category.

Goslin provided a right-handed power bat to complement the left-handed sticks of Greenberg and Charlie Gehringer. He also brought a lighthearted presence to the locker room. Teammate and standout submarine-style pitcher Elden Auker recalled years later that the players appreciated how Goslin kept them loose. "He was some character, a really great guy," Auker said. "He was just happy-go-lucky, always laughing and joking and pulling pranks."[1]

That the club would need only a high level of camaraderie to become pennant contenders seemed far-fetched before the season. The Tigers had not finished closer than 12 games out of first place since 1924, and the positive lineup changes at catcher and left field did not suggest an offensive explosion. But heretofore mediocre hitters such as shortstop Billy Rogell and third baseman Marv Owen, who managed two home runs and 121 runs batted in between them the previous year, combined for 11 blasts and 197 RBIs in 1934 while Greenberg emerged in his second full season as one of the premier sluggers in the sport. The result was that the Tigers led the league with 959 runs scored, one of the highest totals ever during the 154-game era and a whopping 237 more runs than they tallied in 1933.

Some credited Cochrane for lighting a fire under his players. Known as "Black Mike" for his dark moods and legendary temper, he struggled to cope with failure in a game in which failure was inevitable. But that competitive spirit could also prove inspiring. During one game in which his Athletics had fallen far behind the Yankees and had seemingly surrendered, Cochrane began shouting obscenities at his teammates, igniting a comeback that resulted in a victory.

The trio of Goslin, Gehringer, and Greenberg, also known as the "G-Men," did not ride the Tigers to a fast start out of the gate. They stumbled along as expected early in 1934 as only a few thousand fans trickled into home games not featuring the Yankees. But the Great Depression could not stem the tide once the team heated up. The Tigers roared into first place to stay with a 14-game winning streak that lasted until mid-August. The bats sizzled during that stretch to the tune of nearly nine runs per game. Crowds exceeding 30,000 inundated Navin Field to watch the Tigers all but put away the pennant in mid-September with successive defeats of New York.

Among the beneficiaries of the offensive juggernaut were rotation stalwarts Tommy Bridges and 24-year-old Lynwood "Schoolboy" Rowe, whose 24 wins launched a three-year blitz of American League hitters in which he compiled a 62-33 record. But Cochrane, rather than start one of his two aces in Game 1 of the World Series against the Gas House Gang of St. Louis, selected instead former Senators standout General Crowder, who had come highly recommended by Goslin, to match pitches against Cardinals stud Dizzy Dean. The 35-year-old southpaw, who won five of six decisions after the Tigers picked him up off waivers in early August, had not pitched well. He had allowed 81 hits in 66 innings with Detroit—the victories came courtesy of tremendous run support (though he shut out the Yankees in mid-September).

The curious decision backfired when Crowder allowed four runs in five innings, though five Tigers errors played a significant role in the 8–3

Schoolboy Rowe won 62 games for the Tigers from 1934 to 1936.
COURTESY OF THE NATIONAL BASEBALL HALL OF FAME LIBRARY

defeat. Rowe evened the series with a 12-inning masterpiece as a throng of 43,451 at Navin Field watched Goslin single in the game-winner. Daffy Dean, otherwise known as Dizzy's brother Paul, shut down Detroit when the series moved to St. Louis, but wins by Auker and Bridges placed the Tigers on the precipice of a world championship as the clubs returned to the Motor City. Paul Dean outdueled Rowe in Game 6, setting up a showdown for the crown before another huge crowd in Detroit.

It was no contest. Auker, who had hurled a complete-game victory to tie the series, performed horribly on two days' rest. He was knocked out in a seven-run third inning. The chances of his team rebounding from that deficit against Dizzy Dean could be found inside a doughnut. Dean pitched a shutout, leaving the Tigers still seeking their first World Series crown since 1908.

Not even the 11–0 defeat could mar the 1934 season. The franchise had taken a giant leap forward. Cochrane, Goslin, and Gehringer remained viable despite having reached their early 30s, and both Greenberg and Rowe had yet to hit their prime. The demise of the Athletics left only the Yankees as legitimate pennant contenders, and the immortal Babe Ruth had been released to play out the last year of his career with the Boston Braves. The path to another American League championship appeared open to the Tigers.

The G-Men led them down that path. Greenberg, Gehringer, and Goslin combined to drive in 388 runs while Cochrane and promising outfielder Pete Fox both batted over .300 as their team pounded foe after foe into submission. The rotation quartet of Rowe, Bridges, Crowder, and Auker required only proficiency to win 74 games between them.

Not that the 1935 team rocketed from the starting line. All four starters took poundings as the club lost nine of its first 11 to fall seven games behind Cleveland before finding its groove. A 14-4 run followed, but the Tigers pussyfooted around into late June. They rested 7½ games off the pace then warmed with the weather. They sizzled on a 10-game winning streak that included a five-game sweep of the Indians. They won five straight from the Yankees and Tribe on the road to take over first place. A nine-game tear into early August that featured sweeps of Cleveland and Chicago stretched their lead to six games and they never looked back. They needed only to gaze forward—this time to a World Series clash against the Cubs.

The media consensus predicted a Detroit victory. Chicago had lost several players from the 1932 club that had dropped the World Series to New York (which featured the alleged "called" home run by Babe Ruth). Five of its everyday starters had begun the year at age 25 or younger— first baseman Phil Cavaretta was only 18 years old. And some believed that the 21-game winning streak that vaulted it to the pennant had taken a lot out of the team.

The series drew tremendous interest. The Tigers were flooded with so many ticket requests that they were forced to reject some. Both teams built temporary additional seating to accommodate more fans. The night before Game 1 hopeful patrons lined up along Trumbull Avenue outside Navin Field to purchase bleacher seats when the box office opened the next morning. They built bonfires and wrapped themselves in blankets to keep warm. Scalpers the next day were reportedly asking for a then outrageous $25 for tickets that cost them about six bucks. Meanwhile, by order of Detroit school superintendent Frank Cody, kids were excused from classes to listen to the game on the radio from auditoriums. Among the dignitaries at Navin Field that afternoon were actress Greta Garbo, FBI director J. Edgar Hoover, automobile magnate Henry Ford, and, appropriately, Babe Ruth. This was no typical World Series—it was an event.

The crystal ball gazers figured Greenberg would need to bust loose for the Tigers to win. He batted just .253 with two home runs in September but dismissed not only the numbers but those who advised him about how to escape the doldrums. "A half a hundred guys have told me to do this or that in order to get out of the slump," he said. "But I am not going to take their advice, even though I know it was well meant. If I go up there and try to remember what Joe Potatoes or Sam Zilch told me to do, I'll begin to press."[2]

Whatever he did in Game 1 did not work. Greenberg went hitless in three at-bats but received no help from his teammates against Cubs ace Lon Warneke, who hurled a complete-game shutout. Rowe rebounded to perform well after a terrible first inning in which he allowed two runs and committed a costly error. And soon the Greenberg slump would become a moot point. In the seventh inning of a Game 2 victory, after he had blasted a two-run homer through a strong wind in freezing temperatures to cap a first inning in which the Tigers scored four before the first out, Greenberg was hit in the wrist by a pitch. He played out the contest, but despite negative X-rays, swelling prevented him from returning to the Series, though he vehemently protested his absence to Cochrane.

The loss of Greenberg, who had just been named American League Most Valuable Player, required his fellow sluggers and starting pitchers to rise to the occasion. And did they ever. They keyed a critical Game 3 comeback from a 4–1 deficit before a packed house at Wrigley Field. Auker held the Cubs down after falling behind 3–0, allowing consecutive hits by Gehringer, Goslin, Fox, and Rogell in the eighth inning that wrested the lead away. Chicago tied it in the ninth against Rowe, but the Tigers forged ahead in the 11th and Rowe fanned the last two hitters to clinch one of the most dramatic victories in World Series history. "What a battle it was!" Cochrane crowed. "They threw everything they had at us and it wasn't enough."[3]

The 36-year-old Crowder, who proved himself still viable by winning 16 games in the regular season, provided a vintage performance the following day in a taut pitchers' duel against Cubs right-hander Tex Carleton. Crowder allowed only a solo home run to Hall of Fame catcher Gabby Hartnett in a complete-game victory. The Tigers needed just one more win to capture their second world championship.

The Greenberg injury finally came back to albeit temporarily haunt Detroit in Game 5. Lineup replacement Flea Clifton ended it by popping out with runners on second and third and his team trailing 3–1 in the ninth inning. But the Tigers had won two of three in Chicago and had two chances to snag the crown at home.

They only needed one. It was Monday, October 7. A standing-room-only crowd of 48,420 jammed Navin Field to watch the diminutive Bridges, all 155 pounds of him, battle the desperate Cubs. He allowed a two-run homer in the fifth to Billy Herman to fall behind 3–2, but a controversial call in his favor stemmed the tide. Umpire and former Tigers manager George Moriarty ruled Chicago baserunner Stan Hack out at third base after he had attempted to avoid a lunging tag by Clifton. The

Cubs swarmed around Moriarty in protest to no avail—replay in Major League Baseball was still 83 years away.

Bridges weaved in and out of trouble the rest of the way. His greatest Houdini act—with a bit of help from Cubs manager Charlie Grimm—played out in the ninth after Hack slammed a leadoff triple. Bridges fanned Billy Jurges, then Grimm inexplicably, unbelievably, allowed pitcher Larry French to hit for himself. French, who batted .141 that season, dinked a dribbler back to Bridges, who then induced a flyout after Cochrane made a brilliant stop on a pitch two feet in front of the plate. The threat was over. The game remained tied at 3–3.

Soon Goslin was playing hero. A Cochrane hit allowed him to single in the series-clinching run in the bottom of the ninth. It was over. The Tigers had captured their first crown in 28 years. And Bridges received deserved admiration for his gritty performance, including that from Cochrane, who marveled that his pitcher boasted "the heart of a lion."[4]

Added *Detroit Free Press* writer Charles P. Ward: "Those who saw defeat staring the Tigers in the face failed to remember that Bridges is one of the gamest little men that ever came out of the hills of Tennessee. He was sent into the game by Cochrane because Mickey wanted to have somebody on the mound who would show the Cubs plenty of gameness even if he didn't have much on the ball."[5]

A jubilant celebration followed in the locker room and in the streets of Detroit. Cochrane grabbed Bridges and Goslin around their necks and kissed them as newspaper photographers captured the moment. Meanwhile, raucous revelers danced in the streets into the night. They banged on dishpans and gongs as they snaked through Cadillac Square and Grand Circus Park well past midnight while bars remained open to the crack of dawn. Pedestrians walked around and over cars that jammed downtown roads. Police estimated that the partiers outnumbered the group that celebrated the armistice ending World War I in 1918.

The party soon ended literally. And it ended figuratively for the team the following spring. The Yankees were about to end the Detroit reign in the American League, as they did to every club with a temporary hold from the 1920s into the 1960s. And problems for Greenberg and Cochrane—one physical and one emotional—were destined to take a terrible toll on the Tigers.

CHAPTER EIGHT

Fall from Greatness

IT MIGHT BE ASSUMED THAT MICKEY COCHRANE WAS FLOATING ON Cloud Nine as fall turned to winter in 1935. His giddy remarks after he had managed the Tigers to a World Series title indicated such joy. He was a future Hall of Fame catcher who had just established himself as a championship skipper as well.

But raging inside Cochrane was a sea of torment. The same fiery passion that inspired owner Frank Navin to snag him from Philadelphia and place him in charge did not always manifest itself in positive ways. He was overwhelmed by the pressure.

One needed to appreciate his past to understand his present. The intensity with which Cochrane lived his life had been pronounced since childhood. The aspiring Olympic runner often sprinted scared past rural cemeteries late at night near his home in the small Massachusetts town of Bridgewater. He was driven to succeed in all walks of life. Through intense studying and practice on the gridiron he landed a partial scholarship to Boston University, where he emerged as a football star. He even displayed a penchant for heroism when he rescued a teenager who had fallen through the ice. The 160-pound Cochrane, whose comparatively light frame later allowed him to emerge as one of the fastest and most athletic catchers in major-league history, received an opportunity in college to vent his anger and hostility in the boxing ring, absorbing and dishing out punches even against heavyweight fighters.

Nothing had changed by the time Cochrane landed in Detroit, though the physical and emotional wear and tear playing the most demanding position on the diamond resulted in a man who looked well beyond his years. He accepted his job as player-manager with trepidation. He sought tranquility in his life, and his profession certainly promoted neither. He had at one point thrown himself into such pursuits as singing, playing saxophone in a jazz band, and even Shakespearean acting. But by the mid-1930s Cochrane was beginning to break down.

The death of Navin one month after his team finally secured him a crown exacerbated the problem. New owner Walter Briggs added another responsibility to Cochrane's workload, naming him vice president. His mood swings became more pronounced. Those in his professional and personal lives had been alarmed for years about his fits of rage or bouts of sulking and even crying. And in 1936 the strain became overwhelming.

The Tigers were no longer one big, happy family. Dissension crept in after Cochrane convinced Briggs to spend $75,000 to purchase old Philadelphia buddy Al Simmons, a Hall of Fame outfielder discarded by the White Sox after his streak of 11 consecutive .300 seasons with 100-plus runs batted in was broken in 1935. Cochrane believed rightly that Simmons had plenty of gas left in the tank, and his faith proved well-founded when his friend rebounded to hit .327 with 112 RBIs. But his new teammates resented the signing based on money and playing time. Among those most affected was budding superstar Hank Greenberg, who could not land the contract he wanted despite having led the league with 36 home runs and 168 RBIs to win American League Most Valuable Player honors in 1935.

The Tigers never threatened to defend their crown. In late April they lost Greenberg to a fractured wrist sustained in a collision at first base. The addition of Simmons had bolstered their offense enough to overcome the blow, but their rotation lacked depth beyond the indefatigable Tommy Bridges, who led the AL with 23 wins that season. Schoolboy Rowe added 19 victories that proved far more reflective of strong run support than typical performance. He allowed 12 runs in 2⅓ innings in two starts after the death of his father early in the year and never consistently performed well. Meanwhile, foes battered rotation mate Elden Auker, whose earned run average rose over a point from 1935.

The Tigers even slipped under .500 in June. The struggles weighed heavily on Cochrane. Stress led to insomnia. He piloted a plane into the dark night in a desperate search for serenity. But the next day he was exposed again to the grind that ate him up inside. Among his tormenters was *Detroit Free Press* wordsmith Malcolm Bingay, who under the alter ego "Iffy the Dopester" offered that Cochrane was "taciturn, surly, sullen, or boyishly happy as befits his mood and, like a boy, he makes no effort to hide his feelings."[1]

He certainly did not hide his feelings on June 4 after going 0-for-5 in a loss to the Yankees the previous day. He slept nary a wink that night but managed to clobber an inside-the-park grand slam in the third inning. Then it happened. He became so exhausted from insomnia and his sprint around the bases that he almost collapsed as he walked behind the plate after donning the heavy catcher's gear. His heart pounded. Cochrane could take no more. He turned around and made a beeline for the trainer's room. He was diagnosed as on the verge of a nervous breakdown.

Cochrane tried to coach and play through it, but soon doctor's orders prescribed a 10-day isolation at Henry Ford Hospital that placed coach Del Baker at the helm. Visitors were banned from talking baseball. He could not listen to games on the radio nor read about them in newspapers. Such restrictions certainly seemed beneficial to his emotional health when the Tigers embarked on a seven-game losing streak that doubled their deficit behind New York and sent them reeling into sixth place.

Doctors suggested Cochrane remain away from managing upon discharge. Seeking relaxation and peace of mind, he flew with a friend to Montana, then drove to Cody, Wyoming, where he was scheduled to spend a couple weeks resting and fishing. The media arrived to take photos of Cochrane riding on horseback or gently tossing a baseball. He stayed in a secluded ranch that rested in a valley surrounded by mountain cliffs, valleys, and creeks. "It's the greatest place on earth," Cochrane exclaimed.[2]

So much for the short visit. Cochrane extended his "Go West Young Man" trip into mid-July before returning to the Tigers almost exclusively as a manager. He played in five games in August as the club threatened to follow up its world championship with a .500 record. A nine-game winning streak in September prevented that embarrassment, but his mask of invincibility had been removed. Cochrane had been promoted unjustly as indestructible when nobody is. His days in professional baseball were numbered. He would again miss time in 1937 and end his playing career after he was struck in the head by a pitch thrown by Yankees right-hander Bump Hadley, then got fired by Briggs in August 1938. Cochrane eventually embraced a tranquil existence. Though he owned a home in Chicago, he also operated a dude ranch with his father, brothers, wife, and daughter after son Gordon was killed during World War II.

Meanwhile the Tigers played second fiddle to the Bronx Bombers, who despite the end of the Ruthian Era and soon the tragic loss of Lou Gehrig had embarked on what remains arguably the most dominant period in their history.

The temporary collapse of Rowe played a significant role in the inability of Detroit to compete with New York. His comparatively high ERA in 1936 reflected his maddening inconsistency. He managed just one victory over the next two seasons due to pain that trainers attributed to a hard lump on his shoulder and tight muscles. His contentious relationship with Cochrane did not help. The manager suspended Rowe in May 1937 supposedly for being in poor shape, but speculation ran rampant that the Tigers were unjustly probing his personal life.

Rowe rebounded quite well to remain a mainstay in the Detroit rotation after Cochrane gave way permanently to Baker. He thrived in 1940, compiling the best winning percentage in the American League at 16-3, then managed four strong years for the Phillies before and after serving in the military during the war. The big season from Rowe helped the Tigers capture the pennant.

Equally surprising was the performance of 32-year-old right-hander Louis "Bobo" Newsom, who had been acquired early the previous year from the St. Louis Browns. Newsom had wallowed in mediocrity for a decade, leading the league in losses in 1934 and 1935. He then gained the distinction of compiling the worst earned run average in baseball history (5.08) for a 20-game winner in 1938, yet somehow finished fifth in the Most Valuable Player balloting. A three-time 20-game loser in a career that lasted until he was 46 years old, Newsom never managed an ERA under 4.01 until arriving in Detroit. That is where for two seasons he found his groove. He won 21 of 26 decisions in 1940, including 13 consecutive victories, with what was then a career-best 2.83 ERA.

By that time the Tigers had installed another third wheel to the power train in young catcher-turned-first-baseman Rudy York, who remained among the premier run producers in the sport for a decade before alcoholism shortened his career. York, the undereducated product of a small mill town in northwest Georgia, lived haphazardly. Among his unlucky roommates was Billy Rogell, who recalled the experience.

"He was the silliest bastard I ever met in my life," Rogell said. "He was a third-string catcher at the time and I was a regular, and all night long that goddamn phone was ringing. He knew every whore in New York."[3]

High-kicking Bobo Newsom found his groove after arriving in Detroit.
COURTESY OF THE NATIONAL BASEBALL HALL OF FAME LIBRARY

York had a penchant for smoking as he slid into bed at night, starting to booze it up, then forgetting about the lit cigarette in his hand as he fell asleep. "Rudy burned up a couple hotel rooms that way," remembered Greenberg.

He was fine in the batter's box in 1940, posting a career-high .316 batting average and combining with Greenberg for 74 home runs and 284 RBIs. That dynamic duo and the one on the mound featuring Newsom and Rowe played pivotal roles in one of the most exciting pennant races in baseball history as Detroit, Cleveland, and New York battled tooth-and-nail for the crown. The Indians and Tigers waged a back-and-forth struggle for the top through the first half of the season, but the latter appeared destined to place second when they lost 10 of 12 in August to fall 5½ games behind.

Fortunately for the Tigers, dissension was in the process of destroying Cleveland. Indians players despised manager Oscar Vitt, whom they

Slugger Rudy York put his troubles behind him at the plate.

COURTESY OF THE NATIONAL BASEBALL HALL OF FAME LIBRARY

perceived as tyrannical. They eventually publicized their complaints through the media, which reported that they wanted Vitt fired. It all backfired. Vitt kept his job and the 1940 Indians were nicknamed forever as the Crybabies. Soon they collapsed, but the Tigers failed at first to take advantage, losing three straight in Chicago in early September.

A make-or-break series against the Indians in Detroit loomed, and the Tigers rose to the occasion. They outscored Cleveland 28–10 in a three-game sweep during which they bashed seven home runs and nine doubles. Greenberg and fellow outfielder Bruce Campbell, who had spent the previous five seasons with the Indians, terrorized his former team, combining for four blasts among their 11 hits. The set concluded with Detroit a mere half-game behind.

A 26-6 run catapulted the Yankees, who had fallen under .500 in early August, to within one game of the lead before a 2-6 stretch all but doomed their chances. The pennant winner was destined to be determined by six head-to-head battles between the Indians and Tigers to end the season. The clubs entered a three-game showdown in Detroit on September 20 in a flat-footed tie for the top. Tiger fans greeted the Indians mockingly upon their arrival, yelling "Crybabies" at them and trying to stuff baby bottles into their pockets as they scurried by. They booed the Indians unmercifully during the games, which drew 120,000 fans to what had been known as Briggs Stadium since 1938. And they cheered when their team rallied for five runs in the eighth inning against Tribe superace Bob Feller to turn a 4–1 deficit into a 6–4 lead to win the opener.

Detroit took their momentum and ran with it. Rowe pitched a shutout the next afternoon, and though Feller rebounded to win the finale before a throng of 56,771, the Tigers never looked back. They arrived in Cleveland needing just one win and snagged it despite vengeful treatment by Indians fans who threw tomatoes and eggs at them. The win was quite unexpected—Baker opted to pitch minor-league lifer Floyd Giebell against Feller to start the series so that he could keep Rowe and Bridges fresh. Making only his second big-league appearance of the season, Giebell outperformed one of the greatest hurlers of all time in a 2–0 triumph that clinched the pennant. He required only a home run by York to achieve one of the most surprising victories in franchise history.

Giebell was swarmed by his teammates after nailing it down. They carried him off the field and began celebrating in the locker room. But the hero of the day did not join the party. He sat quietly in front of his locker, soaking in the jubilation. His replies to media questions reflected his thoughtfulness. "They thought I should be whooping it up and turning lockers over," he recalled years later. "I didn't feel that way. . . . Something had been accomplished that most boys had dreamed about."[4]

They also dream about playing in a World Series, but Giebell had been promoted too late to be eligible. He performed poorly in sporadic usage in 1941 and never appeared in another major-league game.

He certainly could not have pitched much worse than Rowe or better than Newsom in the Fall Classic against Cincinnati. The Reds knocked out Rowe in the fourth inning of Game 2 and first inning of Game 6, which followed a complete-game shutout by Newsom that featured a three-run homer by Greenberg. The effort that kept Detroit alive was achieved in the wake of his father's death. The usually brusque pitcher showed rare emotion following the victory, retreating to the trainer's room to cry as he avoided reporters. And though Newsom remained unavailable for comment, *Detroit News* sports editor H. G. Salsinger offered that the performance "must be included among all-time classics."[5]

Cincinnati manager Bill McKechnie expressed relief in his thinking that he had seen the last of Newsom. But he had another think coming. Baker decided to start his hottest pitcher in Game 7 on a mere one day's rest. And Newsom performed brilliantly against Reds 20-game winner Paul Derringer. He hurled shutout ball to take a 1–0 lead into the seventh inning before allowing successive doubles and a sacrifice fly to fall behind 2–1. The Tigers managed just one single the rest of the way in dropping a heartbreaker and the series.

The season, however, had been a rousing success. Their attendance of over 1.1 million set a franchise record, and the Tigers appeared destined to remain in contention. But fate stepped in. Military obligations summoned Greenberg in May 1941, then World War II altered the entire landscape for the team and Major League Baseball. The superstar would return just in time to help Detroit provide their fans with another thrill. Based on what he had already achieved, that came as no surprise.

Chapter Nine

The Great Greenberg

THERE WOULD BE NO CHASE FOR IMMORTALITY IN 1938. THE SINGLE-season home-run record of 60 set by Babe Ruth 11 years earlier seemed secure. Tigers slugger Hank Greenberg had powered his way into the realm of possibility, but by September 8 he had blasted only 46. He needed 14 just to tie The Great Bambino with a mere 24 games left on the schedule. It was over.

Or so it appeared. As Yogi Berra later famously uttered, "It's not over 'til it's over." Greenberg embarked on an epic tear. He homered in Cleveland. He clobbered three against the White Sox. He hit three more in a series with the Yankees. He cranked out five during an eight-game stretch, including two against the Indians and Browns. Greenberg had reached 58 with five games remaining. And the baseball world took notice.

His quest advanced no further; Greenberg slammed seven hits, including five doubles, down the stretch but no home runs. And his feat has since garnered far more attention for the social and political ramifications than the physical accomplishment. For Greenberg had come to realize that he was fighting for more than a mark in the record books.

The first superstar Jewish athlete in America had been a target on and off the field throughout his career. Vicious taunts from the dugout and stands based on race or religion were not being saved for Jackie Robinson, who broke the color barrier in 1947. Greenberg, who had previously paid little attention to the frightening rise of anti-Semitic Nazism in Germany, had certainly gained awareness of it during his pursuit of

Babe. "As time went by," he said, "I came to feel that if I, as a Jew, hit a home run, I was hitting one against Hitler."[1]

Major League Baseball—or at least those who played the game—have been accused of working against Greenberg. He received 28 walks in his last 31 games, leading to claims of a desire to prevent a Jew from breaking such a hallowed mark. The allegations rose after he walked 11 times in eight games to start September. But Greenberg finished the season with 119 free passes—18 fewer than Ruth in 1927. And Greenberg refused to believe in a conspiracy, calling it "pure baloney" and later stating that some players and umpires even wanted him to shatter the record.[2]

Such a charge would have been out of character for the classy Greenberg. But that he played in what can kindly be called less politically correct times is undeniable. He and Jewish teammate Harry Eisenstadt were referred to as the "Hebrew Combination" by the *Washington Post*.

Hank Greenberg launching another one of his epic home runs
COURTESY OF THE NATIONAL BASEBALL HALL OF FAME LIBRARY

Greenberg became sensitive to prejudice. He openly supported Robinson in 1947 while finishing his career with the Pirates.

His heritage became a source of pride early in his career. He skipped a game in late September 1934 as the Tigers sought to clinch the pennant because it fell on Yom Kippur, the holiest of Jewish holidays. And as he entered a synagogue the following morning he received a standing ovation from the congregation. He admitted embarrassment by the unexpected show of support. He had, after all, played two weeks earlier on Rosh Hashanah, a celebration of the Jewish New Year, and smashed two home runs against the Yankees.

Greenberg exhibited the same restraint as Robinson did a decade later. He refused to allow the anti-Semites to affect him personally or professionally. But he understood that he had been forced to carry a heavier burden than his peers. "How the hell could you get up to home plate every day and have some son of a bitch call you a Jew bastard and a kike and a sheenie and get on your ass without feeling the pressure?" he asked. "If the ballplayers weren't doing it, the fans were. I used to get frustrated as hell. Sometimes I wanted to go up in the stands and beat the shit out of them."[3]

The son of Romanian immigrants living in Greenwich Village was born on New Year's Day 1911. The couple later moved to the Bronx, where the young Greenberg blossomed into a well-rounded athlete living across the street from the baseball fields of Crotona Park. He embraced the sport, spending hours a day practicing his swing while eager neighborhood kids chased the baseball he slammed great distances.

The boy called Henry did not excel only in baseball. He proved himself an even superior basketball player, excelled in track, and played football despite his comparative distaste for the game. But prospective athletes in the late 1920s certainly considered baseball a more attractive pursuit than basketball, which had barely made a dent as a professional sport.

Not that major-league teams stumbled all over themselves in their quest for Greenberg. The first baseman played a bit awkwardly at 6-foot-4 and 200 pounds. He had not risen to the top of the prospect list in New York, despite having piqued the interest of scouts from the Giants, Senators, Yankees, and Tigers. Only the three American League teams offered a contract. Giants legendary manager John McGraw decided Greenberg did not boast the talent to reach the big leagues. Meanwhile, the Yankees already featured Lou Gehrig at first base, and the Senators were set at that position with perennial .300 hitter Joe Judge. Judge, however, was all but done, and his production as time proved would not compare to that of Greenberg.

That did not result in the Tigers making the best proposal. They offered Greenberg $9,000 to sign—a grand less than the Senators and Yankees. But Greenberg understood that Detroit provided him the best opportunity to succeed. That left the Tigers as the only club interested enough to make a viable proposal. Among its stipulations per the demand of his father was that Greenberg earn his college degree before joining the professional ranks. But son was not tied to the wishes of his dad. He itched to get on with his career, bolting New York University after one year at age 19 in 1930 to be placed into the minor-league system.

Greenberg wasted little time displaying his talent and justifying his signing. He batted .314 with 19 home runs at Class C Raleigh to earn a promotion to Class A Hartford, where he played in 17 games before the curious and struggling Tigers brought him up for the shortest cup of coffee in baseball history. Playing against his hometown Yankees at Navin Field, Greenberg popped out in his only at-bat during a three-week stint.

More important than any lessons learned about baseball during his short stretch with Detroit was a lesson learned about life outside New York, which was the hub of Jewish-American life in the United States. He faced brutal anti-Semitism—and not just from fans or opposing players. After slamming a line drive off the knee of teammate Phil Page upon his arrival in 1930, the pitcher reportedly called him a "goddamn Jew." But fellow Tigers such as Schoolboy Rowe and Billy Rogell provided encouragement. The latter told Greenberg to "go out and outplay the bastards."[4]

Greenberg did just that. But his emergence as a star was not on the immediate horizon. The Tigers, who by that time had successfully groomed slugger Dale Alexander to man first base, decided Greenberg required more minor-league seasoning. He soon established himself as an extra-base-hit machine. He slammed 41 doubles, 10 triples, and 15 home runs at Class B Evansville in 1931 and increased his power numbers the following year, bashing 39 out of the park, with 31 doubles and 11 triples at Class A Piedmont. By that time Alexander had been traded to Boston, and replacement Harry Davis had proven to be merely a mediocre hitter with a dependable glove. The Tigers' starting first baseman job awaited Greenberg in 1933.

Greatness did not. The power that he displayed in the minors abandoned him as he adapted to big-league pitching. Though his average rose steadily after a terrible start, he sputtered along with just two home runs through June, during which he hit none. He showed consistency, keeping his average above .290 from late June forward and finishing the season at .300. But his 12 home runs and 85 RBIs were a far cry from what would become typical.

Few, however, expected the leap Greenberg achieved in 1934. In an era of premier sluggers, he took a backseat to none of them. He not only batted .339 with 26 home runs and 139 RBIs but led the league with 63 doubles, the third-highest total in major-league history and a number that no hitter has since topped. Greenberg was merely warming up. He cranked out 98 extra-base hits in 1935 and led the American League with 36 home runs and 168 RBIs to win Most Valuable Player honors.

The fractured wrist that all but wiped out his 1936 season and some believed threatened his career proved merely a bump in the road. Greenberg returned in 1937 to produce one of the greatest seasons in baseball history. He served notice to the rest of the league with a 17-game hitting streak in May that concluded with a five-hit, two-homer explosion in an 18–3 lambasting of the Browns, raising his average to .378. Most extraordinary was the pace in which he was driving in runs. Greenberg compiled a remarkable 28 RBIs during that stretch with at least one in all but two of those contests.

He continued to knock in his teammates at a prodigious rate and soon threatened the all-time American League single-season record of 184, which had been set six years earlier by Lou Gehrig. A comparative slump in June was followed by a sizzling July in which he drove in 37 runs in 26 games despite hitting just six homers. He added 40 in August to set his sights on Babe Ruth's sidekick, who was still active and thumping.

A 19-game mid-September dry spell in which he recorded multiple RBIs just twice appeared destined to doom Greenberg's quest. He needed eight over the last three games to tie Larrupin' Lou. Fortunately the Tigers had arrived in St. Louis to play the pathetic Browns—Greenberg's personal punching bag. He smashed two home runs and drove in six to pull within two of Gehrig. And in a matchup against 15-0 Indians starter Johnny Allen on the last day of the season, he knocked in the lone run with a first-inning single in a 1–0 Detroit victory to give him 184. He did not bat again with a runner on base.

Greenberg, who wrote in his autobiography that his goal had always been to shatter the record set by Gehrig, had apparently tied it. But future baseball historians scrambled to find discrepancies in his 1937 total and that of Gehrig in 1931. At one point it was decided that Greenberg actually finished with 183, but his official mark remains 184. Statisticians have since determined that Gehrig drove in 185.

Despite the feat, Greenberg received none of the eight Most Valuable Player votes in 1937, finishing third in the balloting behind teammate Charlie Gehringer and an up-and-comer named Joe DiMaggio. He also received nary a one after clobbering 58 home runs in 1938—the practice of voters to reward players on pennant-winners had been established. Greenberg indeed snagged his second MVP in 1940 when he paced the AL with 50 doubles, 41 home runs, and 150 RBIs despite the distraction of moving from first base to left field to accommodate fellow slugger Rudy York, who had been switched from the catching position.

Soon, however, Uncle Sam would hold greater sway than baseball in the life of Greenberg and many of his peers. He was conscripted into the military early in the spring of 1941 after the first peacetime draft in American history commenced the previous fall, costing all but 19 games that season. He could have avoided service after the Detroit draft board deemed him 4F due to flat feet, but he insisted on a reexamination that allowed him to be accepted. He understood the gravity of the war in Europe and Asia and felt a strong sentiment despite the nation's official neutrality. Soon he was inducted into the Army, shrinking his salary from 55 grand annually to 21 bucks a week. "My country comes first," he stated patriotically.[5]

After three months of service Congress ruled men over 28 ineligible for the draft. Having been trained as a tank gunner and risen to the rank of sergeant, the 30-year-old Greenberg was discharged on December 5. But on a fateful morning two days later the Japanese bombing of Pearl Harbor motivated Greenberg to become one of the first major leaguers to enlist. Certainly as a Jewish person he not only felt a motivation to win the war in the Pacific but also a personal drive to defeat Nazism in Europe. He was promoted to first lieutenant after completing officer training school and fought in the Pacific Theater. He finished his stint scouting bombing targets for B-29s. His 47 months in the military during the war proved to be the longest tenure of any ballplayer.

One might have expected Greenberg to be quite rusty or even a shadow of his former self upon his return to the Tigers on July 1, 1945, after having missed four-and-a-half seasons in his prime. But if Athletics pitcher Charlie Gassaway figured as much, he had another figure coming. Greenberg took him deep in the eighth inning, inspiring the sellout crowd at Briggs Stadium to litter the field with their hats—it was hats off to Hank.

The conquering hero did, however, take some time to get back into the "swing" of things. His batting average dipped to .219 after a double-header against the White Sox in Chicago. Then he got hot. Sizzling hot. He slammed 29 hits in just 54 at-bats during a 15-game hitting streak to send the mark skyrocketing to .336.

Greenberg was about to lead the Tigers to their fourth pennant in 12 years. Age finally took a toll thereafter. Though he led the American League with 44 homers and 127 RBIs in 1946, his average dipped to a career-low .277. He was traded that offseason to lowly Pittsburgh, where he concluded his career by batting just .249, though leading the National League with 104 walks.

Dissatisfied with what he perceived as slipshod Pirates management, he retired after the 1947 season. But he was not done with baseball. Best baseball buddy Bill Veeck, the innovative owner of the Indians, named him general manager of that team in 1950. He helped Cleveland win the pennant in 1954 and remain a contender throughout the decade before following Veeck to the White Sox and serving as their part-owner and

GM. What was inevitable had by that time become a reality in 1956 when he was inducted into the Hall of Fame.

Greenberg had also gained a bit of notoriety in 1946 when he married Carol Gimbel, whose family owned the highly profitable New York department store of the same name. The interests of the two clashed—he in baseball and she in art, music, and show horses—but their marriage lasted until their divorce in 1959.

The Tigers recognized arguably the greatest slugger in franchise history on June 12, 1983, when they retired his uniform number 5 (as well as Gehringer's number 2) during a doubleheader against Cleveland. "I am very proud of the fact that my name and uniform will be remembered as long as baseball is played in Detroit," he told the crowd of 34,000 at Tiger Stadium.

Greenberg died of cancer three years later. But his feats on the field will live on forever. Among them was leading his team to the 1945 World Series crown.

Chapter Ten

The Title Team and Beyond

The baseball adage that "You can't tell the players without a scorecard" has never actually been true. The most passionate fans especially have always been aware of at least most guys on the teams they follow. But the closest that old chestnut came to reality was during the latter stages of World War II. Every roster was decimated as more than 500 major leaguers served time in the military from 1942 to 1945.

The result was that some players who normally did not boast the talent to play at that level received an opportunity. Such was certainly the case with the Tigers. With American participation in combat peaking in 1944 and 1945 as the Allies had turned the tide in Europe and Asia, many of their premier players remained engaged in far more important battles. Yet in the second of those years some who indeed required a scoreboard to be identified played significant roles in one of the greatest seasons in franchise history.

The names of the relatively unknown who contributed in 1945 were not exactly considered the who's who of Major League Baseball. Only first baseman Rudy York, all-but-done outfielder Doc Cramer, and decent-hitting journeyman Roy Cullenbine among the position players were known beyond the most ardent baseball followers. Catcher Bob Swift and infielders Eddie Mayo, Skeeter Webb, and Bob Maier (who was playing his only major-league season) were merely hangers-on. The club also felt the loss of outfielder Dick Wakefield, who had led the American League in hits and doubles in 1943 then returned from military duty the following season to help Detroit catapult from seventh place into the pennant race. He did not play in 1945 after agreeing to compete on service teams, yet Detroit outscored all but one American League club that year, greatly because the competition was also fielding lineups of has-beens and the otherwise undeserving.

One advantage for the Tigers was that ace Hal Newhouser had been deemed unfit for military duty when diagnosed with a heart condition called mitral valve prolapse after having been sworn into the Army Air Corps on the mound at Briggs Stadium. His talent proved too great for weaker opposing hitters during the war, particularly after veteran catcher Paul Richards, who entered the scene when new manager Steve O'Neill replaced Del Baker in 1943, became a positive influence on the staff.

Newhouser struggled with his control and emotions on the mound after arriving in the big leagues in 1939. The southpaw managed no winning record in his first four years and even led the league in walks in his

Southpaw Hal Newhouser helped the Tigers win it all in 1945.
COURTESY OF THE NATIONAL BASEBALL HALL OF FAME LIBRARY

first season under O'Neill. But he found his groove the following year and blossomed into one of the most dominant hurlers in the sport. His 29 wins and 187 strikeouts in 1944 paced the junior circuit and resulted in the first of two consecutive Most Valuable Player awards.

A hearing impairment that prevented fellow rotation standout Dizzy Trout from heading overseas allowed him to take a similar path to stardom. The right-hander also learned to control his anger after a mediocre start to his major-league career. He led the American League with 20 wins in 1943 and finished 27-14 the next season with a league-best 2.12 ERA to place second behind Newhouser in the MVP balloting.

The two hotheads were unpopular. Fellow Detroit pitcher Virgil Trucks cited Newhouser as probably his most disliked teammate ever. But they were certainly embraced for their dominance in 1945. The third stud in a dominant triumvirate was relative flash-in-the-pan right-hander Al Benton, who returned from service that year to post a 13-8 record and 2.02 ERA. It was no wonder the Tigers finished that year with the second-best team ERA in the league.

Not that they ran away and hid in the pennant race. Far from it— the return of Greenberg in July proved necessary to vault the club into contention. The Browns and Yankees hung around before fading, but the Senators battled to the end. The Tigers remained in first place most of the season but could not shake Washington, which pulled to within a half-game of the lead in mid-September heading into a five-game showdown with Detroit in the nation's capital. The Tigers began the set with a doubleheader sweep, then hung on for dear life. They lost five of their last eight games, but the Senators fared no better. The Tigers had backed into a World Series showdown against the Cubs.

Nobody cared how they got there. What mattered is that the stars shined. Greenberg, Trout, and Newhouser all rose to the occasion, though the latter required a rebound from an opening-game pounding to play the role of hero.

One late returnee from the war appeared destined to bolster the pitching staff heading into the Fall Classic. That was Trucks, who had won 30 games in 1942 and 1943 combined before leaving. He pitched just once in the regular season in 1945 but made the most of it, performing well in the pennant-clincher, and was deemed ready for the big stage. O'Neill started him in Game 2, and he came through by going all the way in a 4–1 victory that tied the series.

A 3–0 shutout defeat the following afternoon before 55,500 fans at Briggs Stadium proved that the Tigers needed to come alive offensively or they were doomed. And they did, scoring 28 runs in four games the rest of the way as the series moved permanently to hitter-friendly Wrigley Field. Trout performed brilliantly to win Game 4, then Newhouser rebounded from his dud in the opener to take advantage of a three-double effort by Greenberg to place the Tigers within one victory of the championship.

A Game 7 appeared certain when Trucks suffered a fifth-inning knockout the next day. But down 7–1 in the seventh inning against usually steady Cubs starter Claude Passeau, the Tigers staged a spirited comeback. Run-scoring singles by Cullenbine and York closed the gap to 7–3, then a four-run rally in the eighth capped by a Greenberg home run tied it. Enter Trout, who battled against Cubs standout Hank Borowy into the 12th before blinking, allowing a walkoff double to Stan Hack that sent the series into a clincher.

It was no contest. The Tigers clobbered Borowy, whom Chicago manager Charlie Grimm returned to the mound on just one day's rest. He was sent to the showers after recording no outs in a five-run first inning that featured a bases-clearing double by Richards. Newhouser did the rest in a complete game in which he struck out 10. It was time for his team and his city to rejoice.

And rejoice they did. They had celebrated the feats of the boys returning home at the end of the war two months earlier. Now they could exult their baseball heroes. But while a throng was gathering in Detroit to whoop it up, the Tigers were doing the same in their locker room. Among those who wrote about the festive atmosphere was Walter Byers of United Press, who offered the following:

The Tigers roared today. Manager Steve O'Neill's new world champions barged into their dressing room under the Wrigley Field stands . . . and cut loose with the wildest celebration that this ballpark has ever seen for many years. Jammed into the small room with about 40 newspaper men and cameramen, the players, sweaty and dirty, their uniforms half off, pummeled teammates and reporters alike, slapping backs, shaking hands and going nuts in a nice sort of way. An estimated 10,000 fans, band and all, staged an impromptu victory celebration in and around Union Station in Detroit when the Tigers arrived just before 1 a.m.[1]

Streets were packed in the early morning. They were filled by fans waving pennants and tooting horns while the exhausted but appreciative players were whisked through police cordons into taxicabs. An official salute staged by the Detroit Chamber of Commerce the following day allowed participants to dine with their ballplaying heroes at 10 bucks a plate.

Fans besieged ballparks throughout America in the postwar period, and Detroit was no exception. A new optimism about their country fueled by victory overseas and the end of the Great Depression coupled by the love of their championship club inspired a franchise-record 1.7 million to click through the Briggs Stadium turnstiles in 1946. Those who anticipated another crown were disappointed, but nobody could keep up with Ted Williams and the torrid Red Sox that year. The Tigers stumbled along around .500 before catching fire in mid-June and remaining hot the rest of the season. But they had fallen too far behind and finished second.

The trade of York to Boston for weak-hitting infielder Eddie Lake and the questionable relegation of a still-productive Cullenbine to a part-time role had hampered the offense. It certainly promised to worsen when Greenberg was sold to the Pirates a month before spring training in 1947. But astute personnel decisions made by general manager Billy Evans helped maintain his team's status as a winner. Among them was the trade of high-average, no-power outfielder Barney McCosky for future Hall of Famer George Kell. The third baseman batted over .300 in each of his five full seasons with Detroit. He hit .320 with 93 RBIs in 1947, won the AL batting title in 1949, and led the league in both hits and doubles the next two seasons. The Tigers also received four fine campaigns from young outfielder Hoot Evers before he faded.

The result of their contributions and strong years from young pitcher Fred Hutchinson, who lost much of his prime to the war, allowed Detroit to overcome the downgrade of Trout and Trucks into mediocrity (though the latter rebounded for one last strong season in 1949). But it was not enough to raise them back to a championship level. The O'Neill Era bottomed out with a 78-76 record in 1948, leading to his ouster in favor of farm director Red Rolfe. It was a stunning hire. Even the beneficiary was shocked. He knew the club was searching within the organization to find a replacement but never dreamed it would be him.

Evans used a clever ruse to give his new manager the good news. He sidled up to Rolfe and asked, "How would you like to change your office for another one down the hall? The other one's a little bigger. You might like it better." Replied Rolfe: "I'm perfectly satisfied with this office. It's big enough but I supposed I might use a little more space. What office were you thinking of giving me?" Answered Evans: "The one reserved for our new manager."[2]

That new manager and the emergence of 24-year-old slugger Vic Wertz, who racked up 256 RBIs over a two-year period, helped the Tigers vault back into contention in 1950. They joined a pennant race that also featured the Yankees, Red Sox, and Indians. A 20-4 run in May and June that concluded with a three-game sweep of Boston before 120,000 fans at Briggs Stadium catapulted them into first place. They remained in the lead into late August and continued to play well, forging a tie for the top on September 21 after taking three straight from the Athletics. But three consecutive losses in Cleveland while the Yankees were winning five in a row doomed Detroit to second.

Yet optimism abounded. The Tigers boasted several fine young players, which boded well for the future. They appeared destined to remain in contention. But appearances can be deceiving. An era of struggles was about to begin.

CHAPTER ELEVEN

The Collapse and the Comeback

MANAGER RED ROLFE HAD EVERY REASON TO BELIEVE THAT THE everyday lineup that scored 837 runs in 1950 to rank third in the American League would continue to produce the next year. All his position players were either reaching or already in their prime. But he was sorely disappointed, as were Tiger fans who stayed home in droves. The club, which set a single-season franchise attendance record of nearly two million while chasing the pennant, drew more than 800,000 fewer in 1951.

And for good reason. Their team averaged nearly a run less per game. The production of such talent as second baseman Jerry Priddy, Johnny Lipon, George Kell, Johnny Groth, and Vic Wertz dropped dramatically, costing a pitching staff that performed nearly as well many victories. But they were not the biggest culprits. That distinction belonged to outfielder Hoot Evers, who descended from All-Star to easy out. His average dropped from .323 to .224 and on-base percentage fell precipitously from .408 to .297. Evers compiled 103 RBIs in 1950 while leading the league with 11 triples. He drove in 46 the following year with just two three-baggers. Even his defense waned. He totaled six errors in 1951 after committing only one a year earlier.

Among the explanations was his disappointment in contract negotiations. Evers asked Detroit general manager Billy Evans for a raise before the season that would place him third in salary among American League outfielders behind brothers Joe and Dom DiMaggio. He staged a holdout early in spring training before finally signing for $33,000.

The collapse of the Tigers came suddenly, shockingly. They rolled merrily along at 16-10 into early May. They had scored 111 runs during a 12-3 stretch that vaulted them into third place. Then their offense simply disappeared as they dropped permanently out of contention, a status to which they would not return for a decade. During a 1-12 breakdown they averaged 1.8 runs per game. Their 73-81 record that season was tied for their worst since 1931.

But such a mark would have been cause for celebration in the years to come. It triggered a collapse from which the organization would not recover until a new breed of talent arrived and blossomed in the mid- to late 1950s. Evans was dispatched as GM in August 1951 in favor of hometown favorite Charlie Gehringer, who watched in dismay as his club lost its first eight games, plummeting permanently into the cellar on May 2 and falling to 7-21 before he set out to dismantle the ballclub. He traded Evers, Kell, Lipon, and Trout to the Red Sox in what at the time was believed to be a blockbuster deal that returned power-hitting first baseman Walt Dropo, weak-hitting infielders Fred Hatfield and Don Lenhardt, all-but-cooked shortstop Johnny Pesky, and nondescript left-hander Bill Wright. None would last long in a Detroit uniform. Dropo proved particularly disappointing. The former American League Rookie of the Year failed to provide the expected production with the Tigers. The saving grace was that none of the players sent packing performed particularly well for the Red Sox.

The inevitable victim was manager Red Rolfe, who was fired after an Independence Day sweep against Cleveland in which the Tigers were outscored 21–1. The dismissal came as no surprise to Rolfe, who had predicted it years earlier. He had raised the ire of his players after bringing in old Yankees teammate Charlie Keller when he explained, "I signed Keller to give my ballclub some class, Yankee class." And when *New York Times* writer Arthur Daley told Rolfe he was considering picking the Tigers to win the 1951 pennant over the Bronx Bombers, he replied, "Don't do it . . . everyone on our ballclub played over their head last year. Everyone had the best season of his life. I hate to admit it but I can't see us in serious contention. When the Tigers go down, I'll go down with them."[1]

Indeed he did. He was replaced by Fred Hutchinson, who retired as a pitcher to take the job only to return to the mound briefly the following August. He fared no better. The 1952 Tigers finished at 50-104, which remained the worst record in franchise history for more than a half-century. So disheartened had his players become that they lost 13 of their last 15 games.

Strangely, they did the same to start 1953 and threatened to establish themselves as one of the worst baseball bunches ever. The Tigers lost 16 of 17 into mid-June to fall to an eye-popping 11-40 before playing nearly .500 ball the rest of the way to end the year at 60-94. By that time a few newcomers had provided a glimmer of hope, most notably shortstop Harvey Kuenn, who batted .308, led the league with 209 hits, and won American League Rookie of the Year honors, as well as heretofore medi-ocre-hitting third baseman Ray Boone, who arrived from Cleveland early in the season to bat .312 with 93 RBIs in just 385 at-bats.

Their contributions helped the Tigers improve their offense dramat-ically. But their pitching was a mess. Nary a full-time starter boasted an earned run average lower than 4.45 as the rotation had been established as the lousiest in baseball. So Gehringer went to work bolstering the staff.

His efforts on that end proved fruitful through the procurement of veterans. Steve Gromek, who arrived along with Boone in a trade with Cleveland, performed better in 1954 than he had in more than a decade, compiling an 18-16 record and fine 2.76 ERA. Fellow right-hander Ned Garver, who had escaped the lowly Browns, rebounded from a poor first year in Detroit to win 14 and craft a 2.81 ERA. The duo helped the Tigers chop nearly a point-and-a-half off their 1953 team ERA.

But Lady Luck was apparently not a Detroit fan. The work of their vastly improved pitchers was negated by the demise of the offense. Dropo managed just 4 home runs as only two Tigers slugged more than 9. The starting outfield combined for a mere 17. Included was a 19-year-old rookie named Al Kaline, who had landed a spot in The Show without having played any minor-league ball.

Detroit won eight more games in 1954 than it had the year before. But the club finished the season poorly. Hope for the future greatly diminished. The result was another overhaul at the top of the organization.

Among the victims was Hutchinson, who resigned after the 1954 season when the club declined to offer him a two-year contract. The dedicated, foul-tempered skipper refused to accept anything but maximum effort from his players, a tendency that discouraged him more than the losing. He also perceived weakness from umpires, leading to arguments (one of which he started 26 minutes into the first game he managed) that resulted in many an ejection.

"The one thing he demanded was a 100 percent effort, no alibi-ing at all," recalled Kaline. "He was a guy who didn't like to be embarrassed, and

Fred Hutchinson proved to be a better pitcher for the Tigers than a manager.
COURTESY OF THE NATIONAL BASEBALL HALL OF FAME LIBRARY

maybe that one word might be what he really stood for. He wanted his teams to be competitive and not embarrass themselves when they play. If they lose, fine. Lose in the right way. But don't embarrass yourself."[2]

By that time Gehringer had been dispatched. Signs demanding his ouster had popped up around Detroit. He admittedly knew little about the modern landscape in the sport after retiring as a player a decade previous to his August 1951 hire. "I hated the job," he said. "I didn't know who was and who wasn't."[3]

But that did not stop Gehringer from using his position to play swap shop. His trades that sent established standouts such as Kell, Dropo, Trout, Evers, and Wertz could not be greatly criticized because all had regressed and none thrived with their new teams. But one could complain about the bottom line—and Tigers fans certainly did. After all, the club managed a 110-198 record in his two seasons as general manager.

Detroit owner Walter Briggs Jr., who had assumed control of the franchise after the death of his father in January 1952, replaced Gehringer with former journeyman catcher Muddy Ruel, who had served one season as manager of the pathetic Browns but played a role in integrating that team. He had toiled as farm director for both the Indians and Tigers before taking over as GM.

Despite the openness of Ruel to provide an open path to Black ballplayers, the father-and-son Tigers ownerships refused to do the same. Hall of Fame sportswriter Wendell Smith described Walter Briggs Sr. as "Oh, so very prejudiced. He's the major league combination of Simon Legree and Adolf Hitler."[4] It took a threatened boycott of the team more than a decade after Jackie Robinson first appeared in a Dodgers uniform for Detroit to integrate as the second-last major-league team (a year before Boston) to do so. The first step was taken when Dominican infielder Ozzie Virgil joined the club. The first African American to play for the Tigers was outfielder Larry Doby, who had long since been established as a Cleveland star. Fans had to wait until Willie Horton joined the club in the 1960s to enjoy the talents of a homegrown Black standout.

Such mismanagement did not prevent Detroit from rising to the level of mediocrity under veteran manager Bucky Harris, who had guided the Yankees to a World Series title in 1947 before taking over the lowly

Senators for eight years, then returning to the Tigers after having managed that team to five consecutive losing seasons from 1929 to 1933. Behind a blossoming Kaline, a league-best 116-RBI performance from Boone, and a productive season from outfielder and one-year flash Bill Tuttle, the 1955 club paced the American League with 775 runs scored. The revamped pitching staff for which Gehringer deserved credit that was aided by an All-Star effort by young Billy Hoeft and rookie Frank Lary performed respectably enough to help the team finish over .500 for the first time since 1950. Detroit even pulled within the periphery of the pennant race in early August before faltering.

The Tigers did not take their momentum and run with it. They played terribly through the first half of the 1956 season, then heated up well after their fate as an also-ran had been sealed. But more encouraging performers provided hope for the future. Included was always-hustling and popular outfielder Charlie Maxwell, whom Detroit had wisely signed after he had been foolishly waived by Boston. Maxwell batted .326 with 28 home runs and 87 RBIs to earn a spot on the American League All-Star team and launch a fine five-year run with his new club during which he earned a reputation for hitting particularly well on Sundays. He helped the Tigers place second in the AL in scoring as both Lary and Hoeft became 20-game winners and young pitcher Paul Foytack showed promise. Detroit won 32 of its last 46 games in 1956 to be considered by some a future threat to the Yankee dynasty.

The sale of the club in July 1956 from Briggs to a group led by radio and television executives Fred Knorr and John Fetzer also brought optimism and a promise to integrate. It resulted in massive changes, including the promotion of 35-year-old John McHale from director of minor-league operations to general manager and coach Jack Tighe from coach to skipper. But the hope for contention was quickly dashed. Despite the emergence of right-hander Jim Bunning, the 1957 Tigers barely eked over .500, greatly due to the surprising drop in production from Boone, Kuenn, and even Kaline that resulted in an average of one run less per game than in the previous year. Even highly prized second baseman Frank Bolling failed to live up to expectations, a reality that continued through 1960 before he was traded to Milwaukee.

Charlie Maxwell hit well for the Tigers in the late 1950s—particularly on Sundays.

COURTESY OF THE NATIONAL BASE-BALL HALL OF FAME LIBRARY

The Tigers had their claws stuck in the ground, so McHale tried to move them forward through trades in his one season on the job despite claiming the belief that pennants can only be won by improving from within. The revolving door continued to spin. Tighe was fired in favor of minor-league manager Bill Norman after a poor start in 1958. He performed well in his duties, but a 2-13 launch the next season ended his tenure and motivated the Tigers to place him with veteran manager Jimmy Dykes. Meanwhile, the resignation of McHale resulted in scouting director Rick Ferrell taking over as GM in 1959 as the club on the field remained mediocre.

A new decade approached. And things were about to get quite interesting.

CHAPTER TWELVE

"Cashing" In and Landing
a Piece of The Rock

It was April 17, 1960. Immensely popular Cleveland slugger
Rocky Colavito had reached first base on a force play in inning four of
the last exhibition game of the season when he was approached by manager Joe Gordon. The man who led the American League in home runs
in 1959 and was revered by Indians fans as "The Rock" was informed he
had been traded to Detroit.

Colavito figured at first that Gordon was joking. After all, he was
beloved in his adopted city, particularly among those in the Italian-
American community. But soon reality set in. Indians general manager
Frank "Trader" Lane had indeed shipped him off in exchange for singles
hitter Harvey Kuenn with the explanation that power is overrated. Lane
cited the Senators, who had ranked second in the American League in
home runs the previous year and second-last in runs scored. What he
failed to realize or refused to mention was that premier Washington sluggers Harmon Killebrew, Jim Lemon, and Bob Allison, who combined for
105 home runs in 1959, were surrounded by terrible hitters. They were
not the problem.

It did not matter anymore. While Cleveland fans protested vehemently and what became known as "The Curse of Rocky Colavito"
launched that franchise into the longest run of noncontention in major-
league history, the handsome and hardworking right fielder became a
mainstay in a Detroit uniform. "Our biggest need now is to score more

Rocky Colavito consistently hit for power in the early
1960s after arriving from Cleveland.
COURTESY OF THE NATIONAL BASEBALL HALL OF FAME
LIBRARY

runs and we feel Rocky will help us more than Harvey in that respect,"
offered Tigers president Bill DeWitt.[1]

General manager Rick Ferrell certainly knew whom to call when
seeking a robbery. He had five days earlier ripped off Lane in a swap that
dispatched third baseman Steve Demeter, whose entire career consisted
of 23 at-bats, and landed first baseman Norm Cash, who exploded into
greatness in 1961 and remained one of the most consistent sluggers in the
sport as a Tiger for 15 seasons. So infatuated was Lane with making deals
that he actually swapped managers with Detroit, sending Joe Gordon in
return for Jimmy Dykes in early August 1960. Both were fired by 1962.

The additions of Cash and Colavito did not immediately send the
Tigers soaring to the heights. DeWitt was inaccurate when he claimed

that their most pressing need was offense. His team had finished third in the American League in runs scored in 1959 and struggled with one of the worst rotations in the sport despite a fine season from Don Mossi, who had arrived from Cleveland a year earlier and made a successful conversion from reliever to starter. And indeed, at least in 1960, Lane appeared justified in his criticism of power as a primary weapon. Detroit ranked second in the AL with 150 home runs but dropped to seventh in runs. The club compiled a 71-83 record even with an improved pitching staff which overcame a shoulder injury that sent the career of Paul Foytack reeling.

Norm Cash became an integral part of a powerful lineup in the 1960s.
COURTESY OF THE NATIONAL BASEBALL HALL OF FAME LIBRARY

That season did not promote hope for the future. The value of the Colavito trade remained in question when his production fell from previous years. The simple lesson learned was that a powerful offense requires contributions throughout the lineup, and great teams must boast a strong and deep pitching staff.

Welcome to the 1961 Tigers. That they hired as manager Bob Scheffing, who was coming off three losing seasons as skipper of the Cubs, was unexpected. That Cash led the league with a .361 average with 41 home runs and 132 RBIs—numbers in all categories he would never again match—was shocking. That Colavito cranked out career-bests in home runs (45) and RBIs (140) surprised the baseball world. That rookie third baseman Steve Boros compiled a .381 on-base percentage and drove in 62 runs despite missing five weeks with a broken collarbone raised eyebrows. But that Ferrell could lure three viable players in a trade with Milwaukee for phenom-turned-mediocrity Frank Bolling proved to be perhaps the most stunning development of all. Catcher Dick Brown, outfielder Bill Bruton, and lights-out reliever Terry Fox all played major roles in success the level of which few could possibly have anticipated.

Indeed, Detroit led the American League in runs scored while the trio of Jim Bunning, Mossi, and Frank Lary, who ended a seven-season run of greatness with a 23-9 record before a sore arm wrecked his career, combined for 55 victories. And fans came out in droves to watch the team. More than 1.6 million showed up at newly named Tiger Stadium, and they were rewarded most of the season with a pennant race.

A road sweep of the White Sox helped Detroit win 17 of its first 22 games and take a three-game lead over the competition. They attracted more than 100,000 in back-to-back defeats of New York in mid-June to again wrest the lead away. They spent most of the spring and early summer in first place before the powerful Yankees took over the top spot in late July.

But the Tigers continued to win and pressure the Bronx Bombers. They rested a mere 1½ games behind when they invaded the Big Apple for a Labor Day weekend showdown in sizzling temperatures. A throng of 65,566 packed Yankee Stadium for the opener, and those who loved pitching duels were not disappointed. Mossi and New York ace Whitey

Ford, who departed in the fifth inning with tightness in his hip, pitched shutout ball that continued on both sides into the ninth. Extra innings appeared inevitable when Mossi retired the first two batters. But singles by Elston Howard, Yogi Berra, and Moose Skowron tamed the Tigers. A Colavito home run gave them a two-run lead in the second game of the series, but Lary could not hold it. Detroit tried to salvage the finale and led 5–4 in the ninth, but after a Mickey Mantle blast tied it, reliever Ron Kline surrendered a three-run homer to Howard that completed the sweep.

The Tigers never recovered. Their losing streak reached eight as they scored just 17 runs in the process, ballooning their deficit to 10 games as the Yankees ran away from the pack and heightened the national attention on the battle between Mantle and Roger Maris to break Babe Ruth's single-season home-run record. Detroit was doomed but continued to fight, winning 10 of its last 12 to finish at 101-61, matching the highest victory total in franchise history, securing its best record in 27 years, and earning the rare distinction of reaching triple figures in wins and not placing first. It would not be done in the American League for another 19 years.

But just as had happened a decade earlier, when the Tigers won the same number of games, everything had broken right and the club did not boast the pitching nor hitting depth to remain pennant contenders. A painfully slow start by Colavito, who batted under .200 and did not homer until mid-May, along with a sore arm that doomed Lary to a permanent career collapse, sent them reeling in 1962. They heated up with the weather to pull within a game of first place in early June and stayed in the race for another month before a 3-11 stretch that included sweeps in Chicago and Los Angeles wrecked their chances. Only a late-September surge assured them of a winning record.

A similar scenario continued to play out into the mid-60s, but with a different cast of characters running the organization. Sole owner John Fetzer promoted to GM in 1963 longtime employee Jim Campbell, who wasted little time after a slow start that year firing Scheffing and replacing him with venerable Chuck Dressen, who had begun his managerial career with the 1934 Cincinnati Reds, won two pennants with the defunct Brooklyn Dodgers, and had lost his job with Milwaukee two years earlier.

It has been offered that a team often takes on the characteristics of their manager, and such proved to be true of the Tigers under Dressen, a fiery sort and baseball lifer (though he played quarterback briefly for the NFL Decatur Staleys) who put his heart and soul into his job, studying the science of the sport and even taking pride in his ability to steal signs. He believed his knowledge of baseball and strategic strengths compared to that of less experienced skippers could mean the difference between winning and losing close games.

And the Tigers won under Dressen—just not enough to threaten eventual pennant winners. His players responded almost immediately after a 10-game losing streak had already destroyed their 1963 season and sent Scheffing packing. A 21-7 run in July nearly pushed them back to .500.

Dressen felt he could transform the Tigers into contenders again, but the fans were skeptical. Attendance dropped under one million in 1963 for only the second time since World War II and remained under that mark the following year. But the fans who stayed home in 1964 missed out on a far more balanced offense that featured several young players who would eventually vault the team into greatness. Included were catcher Bill Freehan, power-hitting shortstop Dick McAuliffe, third baseman Don Wert, and pinch-hitter extraordinaire Gates Brown. Meanwhile, blossoming southpaw Mickey Lolich was on the verge of providing the staff with a much-needed ace and right-hander Denny McLain had begun to make his mark. It even appeared that veteran Dave Wickersham, who compiled a 19-12 record in 1964 after arriving via a trade from Kansas City that shipped off Colavito, would be a mainstay atop the rotation. But he struggled thereafter and was gone by the magical 1968 season.

Foot and knee injuries that limited the production of Kaline hindered the Tigers in their quest to contend in 1964. Then the 70-year-old Dressen suffered a heart attack the following spring. He was left in a weakened condition and replaced by Bob Swift, then returned in May. Campbell continued to build what would be a champion by adding to the everyday lineup its first Black star in Willie Horton, who paced the team with 104 RBIs, while Dressen provided some playing time for fellow outfielders Jim Northrup and Mickey Stanley. But the 1965 staff still lacked depth behind Lolich and McLain, a deadly shortcoming in what was rapidly emerging as an era of pitching dominance in Major League Baseball. The result was that Detroit hung around the pennant race for a while but could not keep pace with the steamrolling Minnesota Twins.

The same destiny awaited the Tigers in 1966. The difference was that they spent most of that season without Dressen, who sustained a more powerful heart attack than the first one, then fell victim to a kidney infection while recuperating. And on August 10 a fatal heart attack took his life at age 71. "Few remain in baseball who can match his deep knowledge and sincere enthusiasm for the game," eulogized Tigers owner John Fetzer.[2]

The club won nearly 90 games in both 1965 and 1966, but pennant contention in August and September remained a pipe dream—balanced Baltimore ran away and hid in the second of those seasons. But Campbell added what might be considered the final piece of the puzzle in June 1966 when he put on a mask and robbed the Red Sox of right-hander Earl Wilson, who joined Lolich and McLain to form a formidable threesome and only cost the Tigers fading utility man Don Demeter.

The Tigers were ready to roar. The social and political upheavals of the times were capturing far more attention from Detroiters. But their baseball team was about to provide a much-needed escape and bring a violence-battered city together.

Chapter Thirteen

A Title for Tiger Town

Tigers general manager Jim Campbell did not race to the phone to call Mayo Smith and offer him the managerial position after a 1966 season during which both Chuck Dressen and interim replacement Bob Swift died.

Smith was not even on Campbell's radar. He sought to hire Al López, who had never compiled a losing record in 15 years as Indians and White Sox manager.

Strike one. López had been ill and wanted to wait a while before returning to the game, which he did with Chicago in 1968.

Campbell then tried to lure former Yankees manager Ralph Houk to the job.

Strike two. Houk was not far removed from winning World Series crowns with that club and decided to stick around despite having fallen into last place the previous year.

Then Campbell set his sights on Bill Rigney, who had yet to place higher than third in 11 years with the Giants and Angels but had won American League Manager of the Year honors in 1962.

Strike three. Rigney wanted to remain in sunny California.

Campbell yearned for an experienced skipper. So he turned to Smith, whose Philadelphia and Cincinnati clubs of the 1950s were steeped in mediocrity and had never recorded a winning season. He had since been strongly rumored to land several managerial posts but came up empty every time. Smith snagged the job in Detroit practically by default.

The Tigers would not regret it despite occasional displays of disrespect from his players—Norm Cash was quoted as complaining that Smith was the "dumbest manager in baseball."[1] He certainly made one smart move upon his arrival when he switched Dick McAuliffe from shortstop to second base, where he emerged as an All-Star.

Smith proved himself a departure from those previously at the helm. He was far more cool-tempered and worked to empower his players to maximize their talents. Longing to earn their immediate trust, he contacted Al Kaline and Bill Freehan, as well as other Tigers during the Winter Meetings. He had a reputation for indecisiveness during his previous regimes, so he felt the need to gain the confidence of his talent, even before spring training.

The makeup of the club had long been established. The young hitting and pitching standouts were ready to take the next step forward and join the veterans in an effort to contend. Fortunately for Detroit there would prove to be no dominant team in the American League in 1967. That helped. The result was the tightest and arguably most thrilling pennant race in baseball history.

The Tigers were far from a perfect team. Shortstop Ray Oyler could not hit a lick. Promising center fielder Mickey Stanley struggled at the plate all season and finished at .210. The rotation and bullpen proved mediocre. A penchant for surrendering longballs plagued Earl Wilson and Denny McLain, resulting in Detroit allowing the most home runs in the AL. But there were far more positives than negatives. Willie Horton, Kaline, Freehan, McAuliffe, and Stanley all slammed at least 19 home runs, outfielder Jim Northrup continued to emerge as a batting threat, and Wilson came through with his finest season in baseball, posting a record of 22-13 despite his propensity for surrendering bombs.

Two sweeps of Baltimore, which had surprisingly collapsed after capturing the World Series the previous year, catapulted the 1967 Tigers into first place. They remained hot into early June, raising their record to 31-18 to stay atop the American League standings. A 7-16 stretch in which the hitters and pitchers took turns collapsing pushed Detroit 5½ games behind the White Sox, whose first slump was right around the corner. The Tigers still could not hit their stride. A seven-game winning

Willie Horton led the world champion Tigers in home runs in 1968.
COURTESY OF THE NATIONAL BASE-BALL HALL OF FAME LIBRARY

streak was followed by a seven-game losing streak. They fell into fifth place in mid-July yet only 3½ games out of first as an incredible pennant race took shape.

The calming effect of Smith prevented the Tigers from panicking. He worked to keep their confidence raised and looking hopefully forward to success rather than dwelling on past failures.

Then it happened. It was 3:45 a.m. on July 23 when bottles and rocks were thrown at police who had raided an unlicensed drinking club on the near west side of Detroit. The fracas in the wee hours of the morning escalated into rioting, which had become disturbingly common through-out the nation in the mid-1960s. Mayor Jerome Cavanaugh stunningly convinced the local media to refrain from reporting on the violence. The result was that the 34,623 fans who poured into Tiger Stadium that afternoon to watch a doubleheader against the Yankees knew nothing about the increasingly deadly battles ongoing a mere three-and-a-half miles north.

They learned soon enough. Among those given a panoramic view was *Detroit News* sports columnist Pete Waldmeir, who spoke of his experiences decades later. "I remember pulling into the players' parking lot around 11:30 a.m. and Carl, a Detroit street cop who worked there quite a bit, had a dark hat on and not the white one I usually saw, which was kind of strange," he recalled. "When we got out of the car, he says: 'What are you doing here, don't you know there's a riot going on?' I, of course, had no idea. He says: 'Come with me.'"[2]

The officer escorted Waldmeir to the roof of the stadium where he could see smoke billowing up from the riot area and was warned to avoid driving on the freeway heading home because of the threat of snipers.

Among those who noticed the city burning over the left field and center field third deck were Tigers radio announcers Ernie Harwell and Ray Lane, who at first figured someone might be burning tires. But around the second inning engineer Howard Stitzel called with a demand from Campbell not to mention what they saw on the air. The pair did not question the edict.

The insurrection forced the Tigers to postpone their home games against the Orioles and play them in Baltimore later in the week. Far more critically it cost the lives of 43 people and proved to be one of the deadliest riots in American history. The baseball team was needed more than ever as a diversion (Horton made a locker-room plea to the citizenry for the violence to stop during the unrest) and an outlet to help bring the smoldering city back together.

But it seemed the Tigers were spinning their wheels. The four-team race prevented them from taking control. They won 10 of 13 games in mid-August and gained only one game in the standings as a third-place club. They spent early September behind Boston, Chicago, and Minnesota, yet stood only 1½ games off the lead. A sweep of lowly Kansas City and a four-game winning streak catapulted them to the top on the 16th. It was nip-and-tuck down to the wire.

A series at Tiger Stadium against California was scheduled to conclude the regular season, but a playoff was a strong possibility. A double and homer by Willie Horton keyed a victory in the first game of a Sunday doubleheader before nearly 40,000 fans and placed Detroit on the precipice of a one-game showdown against Boston for the pennant.

The season hinged on a strong performance by McLain. He had struggled mightily in September and lost two weeks to a toe injury he claimed was sustained when he stubbed them racing to deal with raccoons who had invaded his garbage cans at home. He later changed his story several times—it was the first noteworthy indication that McLain was not playing with a full deck or had become involved with gamblers. He got knocked out early in the nightcap after a home run by Northrup and triple by McAuliffe provided him a 3–1 lead, and the Tigers were doomed. The Angels battered the bullpen as well, then McAuliffe ended all hopes by hitting into just his second double play of the season—both in the last five games. What became known as The Impossible Dream had turned into a reality for the Red Sox, who secured the American League crown after finishing second-last in 1966.

"I hope we get another chance to do it next year," said Freehan wistfully. "We have nothing to be ashamed of this year. A couple of big innings were all we needed. But you can't cry over what's past. The games we lost in May and June hurt as much as the two we lost this weekend. Just one big inning; that's all we needed."[3]

Added Kaline about the future of his club: "We now know we have a good ball club and know what has to be done. It was a loss but it was a tremendous experience for us. Every man here hopes he gets another chance to do it next year."[4]

They did. Campbell virtually stood pat in the offseason in the belief that his team boasted the talent and now the experience in a playoff race to win the pennant. The Year of the Pitcher approached and Detroit could match arms with any team in the American League. It could also claim the most potent offense in baseball, which was not saying much in 1968. The Tigers in fact scored fewer runs that year than they had in 1967. The increase in production from Horton and Northrup was offset by the decrease from the aging Kaline, who lost time to a broken arm and was otherwise relegated to part-time duty.

One huge difference was McLain, who blossomed from decent to dominant, winning the first of two consecutive Cy Young Awards before his career and life were ruined by his buffoonish behavior. He found his groove as a crafty right-hander who kept hitters off-balance. His strikeout total skyrocketed from 161 to 280 in 1968 in earning what could be the distinction (given the carefulness in which starting pitchers are handled in the modern era) of becoming the last 30-game winner in baseball. McLain cut his earned run average nearly in half from the previous year while rotation mates Lolich, Wilson, and Joe Sparma maintained their dependability.

The Tigers ensured their fans by mid-June there would be no pennant race that year. They had bolted into first place a month earlier and took control for good with a four-game sweep of the Twins in which the pitching staff held their typically hard-hitting foe to five total runs. Detroit never looked back. Its lead shrunk to four games in late August, but it responded with a 10-2 run that ended any suspense. The Tigers, who exceeded two million in attendance for the first time in franchise history, awaited a World Series clash against defending champion St. Louis, which had run away from its National League competition.

Stories abounded as the team prepared for the showdown. Among them was longing for a title in Detroit, which was still recovering from the devastating riot of the previous summer. The Tigers had already helped bring the city together, but it was understood that a Fall Classic crown could complete the job. Another headline was an anticipated pitching matchup between McLain and fellow Cy Young Award winner Bob Gibson, who dazzled the opposition in 1968 with a 1.12 earned run average that still stands as the greatest in modern baseball history. Gibson had nearly single-handedly won the 1967 Series by taking three games from the Red Sox and had proven himself even more dominant in 1968.

Those who expected taut battles between McLain and Gibson were in for a letdown. But those who anticipated a thrilling series were not. Gibson threatened to repeat his performance of a year earlier when he hurled a complete-game five-hit shutout in the opener. And while Gibson was establishing a World Series record that still stands with 17 strikeouts, McLain collapsed in the fourth inning and forced Smith to remove him for a pinch-hitter in the sixth.

Lolich then planted the seeds for his heroism. Before a second straight sellout crowd at Busch Stadium, he shut down the Cardinals and even recorded one of three Tiger home runs in evening the series. His stellar pitching grew in necessity when St. Louis won the next two in Detroit, including a Game 4 in which Gibson cruised against a battered McLain, who could not even make it out of the third inning.

The Tigers were on the verge of defeat. Then the pitcher called affectionately by some The Fat Man for his rather rotund midsection rose to the occasion again. Lolich overcame a 3–0 deficit in Game 5 to hurl shutout ball the rest of the way and take advantage of huge RBI singles by Kaline and Cash to keep his team alive.

Smith had a dilemma. He chose to pitch his two aces on two days' rest, but that meant starting McLain in Game 6, who had performed horribly. The good news was that St. Louis manager Red Schoendienst opted to hold Gibson for a potential deciding battle. The strategy worked for the Tigers. McLain found his rhythm and could relax as his teammates pounded Cardinals starter Ray Washburn, who had stymied them in Game 3. The heart of the lineup smashed balls all over Busch Stadium. Kaline, Cash, Horton, and Northrup combined for 10 hits—the bookends of that quartet both homered in the 13–1 triumph.

Game 7 promised a Clash of the Titans on the mound. Most believed the unhittable Gibson boasted an advantage, particularly in his home ballpark. But Lolich matched him pitch for pitch and goose egg for goose egg through six innings. The seemingly unflappable Gibson, who had allowed just one hit, retired the first two batters in the seventh before Cash and Horton singled.

A crack had finally appeared in his armor and, to make matters worse for the Hall of Famer, up to the plate strode Northrup, who had homered off him in Game 4. Northrup nailed a first-pitch fastball, sending a line drive to center field, territory usually roamed expertly and speedily by Curt Flood. But Flood, who would gain greater fame spearheading the movement for player freedom, broke in on the ball, then slipped as it flew over his head. The mistake cost two runs, which might have seemed like 10 given how Lolich was pitching. And when Freehan doubled in Northrup, the fat lady began to sing.

Catcher Bill Freehan and winning pitcher Mickey Lolich celebrate the clinching of the 1968 crown.
COURTESY OF THE NATIONAL BASEBALL HALL OF FAME LIBRARY

A Mike Shannon home run with two out in the ninth spoiled the shutout, but it did not matter. The Tigers and their fans could celebrate. They both did with relish—20,000 Detroiters greeted their heroes at the airport. But the victory meant more than a championship to Lolich. The World Series Most Valuable Player had not only won thrice but had stepped out of McLain's shadow. And it felt great. "Mickey Lolich has always been a number on the roster," he crowed. "Finally, somebody knows who I am."[5]

Far more important was the impact the Tigers made on the city 15 months after it had been torn apart figuratively and literally by racial strife. "For one brief, shining moment after Detroit won the American League pennant, blacks and whites mingled in color-blind joy, thousands strong, on the streets of downtown Detroit," offered the *Free Press*.[6]

And when the team snagged the World Series crown, an even more raucous celebration proved that its meaning extended far beyond a baseball achievement. Wrote legendary local sports columnist Joe Falls in the *Sporting News*: "My city needed a release; it needed an outlet to release its pent-up emotions. It found it in a baseball team, men playing a boy's game."[7]

Owner John Fetzer reportedly expressed it more succinctly to Smith. "You've not only won the pennant and the series," he said. "You might have saved the city."[8]

Fetzer was referring to the entire organization. But one player who received a bit less of an opportunity to contribute during the regular season had performed particularly well. And that was Kaline, who in his first chance to shine in World Series competition rose to the occasion by batting .379 with two homers and eight RBIs. And he continued to prove wrong those who assumed that in his mid-30s he was ready to be put out to pasture. Kaline was about to cement his legacy as one of the greatest all-time Tigers.

CHAPTER FOURTEEN

Mr. Tiger

TIGER FANS PRIVILEGED ENOUGH TO HAVE WATCHED AL KALINE IN action should give thanks daily to a right-handed pitcher named Tom Qualters. And to the Philadelphia Phillies.

Qualters, who in the eye of the Tigers was born appropriately on April Fool's Day, proved so attractive as an amateur pitcher in the early 1950s that the Fightin' Phils signed him to a contract, beating out Detroit in the competition for his services. So the Tigers went after whom they perceived as the next-best player available. And that was Kaline.

No comparison. Qualters pitched in 34 major-league games without registering a decision or save. Kaline blossomed into a Hall of Famer.

Albert William Kaline was born six days before Christmas in 1934 and raised in a poor section of Baltimore. His parents struggled to make ends meet—his father was a broom maker and mother scrubbed floors— but they never forced their son to contribute financially by taking on a job. Kaline carried with him throughout his life an appreciation for their selflessness. "They'd always helped me," he said. "They knew I wanted to be a major leaguer and they did everything they could to give me time for baseball. I never had to take a paper route or work in a drugstore or anything. I just played ball."[1]

That gratitude motivated Kaline to pay off their mortgage and spring for his mother's eye operation upon receiving a reported $35,000 bonus from the Tigers after Qualters had been snatched by Philadelphia in 1953. He earned it through his feats at Southern High School and determination to overcome osteomyelitis, a chronic bone disease that forced doctors to surgically remove a bad bone from his left foot, causing Kaline to run abnormally throughout his career.

Kaline boasted an incredible arm that he first displayed at a picnic festival as a child by unleashing a baseball 173.5 feet. So taken aback were the judges that they ordered him to toss another one to ensure the

Al Kaline enjoyed a long and illustrious career with Detroit.
COURTESY OF DREAMSTIME

accuracy of the measurement. The result was a 175-foot heave. Kaline had built up his arm strength firing pitches to his father, a former semipro player. The boy had developed a fastball, curve, and changeup by age nine, resulting in a dominant run for his grammar school club.

He was not long for the mound. His high school team was set with pitchers when he arrived as a freshman, so he was moved to center field with the plan to learn that position before promotion to the varsity as a sophomore. Kaline tore up that blueprint with his talent. He started for Southern in his first year and batted .333, then .418 the following year to pique the attention of major-league scouts. He was selected to play in an annual all-star game at the Polo Grounds in New York during which he smashed a home run and two singles to earn the Lou Gehrig Trophy given to the most valuable player.

Kaline continued his rapid rise. Not only did he flirt with a .500 batting average as both a junior and senior, but he began to excel in the outfield and show off the arm that would eventually become legendary.

Among those who considered Kaline an ideal prospect was Tigers scout Ed Katalinas, who had already signed Vic Wertz and Paul Foytack and would eventually land fellow standouts Bill Freehan, Mickey Lolich, Willie Horton, and Denny McLain. "To me he was the prospect that a scout creates in his mind and then prays that someone will come along to fit the pattern," Katalinas said of Kaline, who bolstered his status by batting a remarkable .609 in one season of American Legion ball.[2]

Katalinas had first spotted Kaline as a skinny 15-year-old second baseman whose lack of power was offset by his calm and patient approach at the plate and speed running the bases. The scout had arrived to check out another player but soon turned his attention to Kaline. "He was one of the golden boys," Katalinas told *Sports Illustrated* in May 1956. "The moment I saw Kaline I forgot all about [his original target]. After the game I spoke to the kid and introduced myself. The poise came through in conversation too. He was shy, always has been, but there was no doubt about what he wanted to do. He wanted to play baseball, period."[3]

The Tiger bird dog continued to follow Kaline, who eventually emerged as the most sought-after high school talent in Baltimore. The kid added weight and power. His desire to play became insatiable. His baseball-mad uncles drove him from high school games to American Legion games to recreational league games, sometimes all in the same day. Kaline changed uniforms in the car. Soon Katalinas shouldered some of the driving load in the hopes of currying favor and eventually signing Kaline. It was no cakewalk to a marriage. He had piqued strong interest from other teams, particularly the Cardinals.

The Tigers certainly required a talent upgrade after their 104-loss season in 1952. But more than a decade before the advent of the amateur draft they were required to outbid the competition for Kaline's services. Team president John McHale preferred Qualters, but his acquisition by the Phillies freed up money to sign Kaline. The executive felt secure in giving his permission after traveling to Baltimore to watch Kaline play in amateur competition. The Tigers had to wait under major-league rules until after Kaline graduated from high school. A day after the ceremony Katalinas visited the Kaline home and offered a bonus and contract that totaled $30,000.

Little could anyone have imagined that within months he would launch a career as a Tiger that would never be interrupted by even a short stint in the minors. His emergence played arguably the most significant role in transforming the Tigers from patsies to respectability by the middle of the decade.

One could not have known what to expect from an 18-year-old with no professional track record. That he landed a starting role in 1954 and batted a respectable .275 with four home runs did not raise many eyebrows despite his rebound from the first of many injuries, a twisted knee when he hit the wall running hell-bent after a foul ball. But that at age 20 he nearly placed second in the American League Most Valuable Player voting after leading one and all with 200 hits and a .340 batting average was stunning. He hit safely in 25 of his first 26 games in 1955, including a three-homer explosion against Kansas City during which he blasted two in the same inning, and appeared destined to win the MVP award until a September slump.

The youngest batting champion in baseball history started slowly in 1956. He managed just eight home runs through June 29, and his average dropped to .265 a week later. Kaline then sizzled with three consecutive three-hit games that launched a month-long tear during which he batted .406 with 11 home runs and 42 runs batted in, more than one per game. He finished the season with what would remain a career-high 128 RBIs.

Kaline only once more (in 1963) reached triple figures in that department. Several factors weighed into his inability to maintain that level of production despite spending most of his career batting in the primo third or fourth positions in the batting order. One was his tremendous patience at the plate which, combined with the tendency of pitchers to work around the dangerous hitter, resulted in high walk numbers and on-base percentages. Kaline finished his career with a .376 OBP.

Another major factor was injuries. He rarely missed long stretches, but nagging physical problems often kept him out of the lineup, particularly from 1967 forward. Kaline did not again play in more than 133 games until his retirement season of 1974.

Kaline also competed in a pitchers' era. Few hitters consistently compiled triple figures in RBI—teams were simply not placing enough runners on base to make it possible. Kaline even led the American League in slugging percentage in 1959 despite hitting just 19 doubles and 27 home runs. The Tigers barely scored four runs per game in their 1960s heyday, yet remained atop or near it in the AL in that category.

Various distractions also contributed. Kaline suffered through a terrible 1960 season after a business partner convinced him to buy racehorses for tax purposes. Such a purchase was considered bad form for ballplayers because of the connection between horse racing and gambling. Though no legitimate finger of accusation was pointed at Kaline, he was still forced to sell his interest in the stable.

Kaline never gained the recognition earned by the premier outfielders of his era. Though he could not continue to match the production of the greatest of his generation such as Mickey Mantle, Willie Mays, and Hank Aaron, his numbers and all-around brilliance ranked him among those at the next level, including the great Roberto Clemente. The two were sometimes compared not just for their statistical similarities but also their defensive prowess and powerful arms. It was no wonder Kaline earned 17 All-Star berths and eight times was placed among the top 10 in MVP voting.

He also remained viable well into his late 30s. Though limited to just 278 at-bats in 1972, he played a significant role in his team's run to the playoffs by hitting .313 with 10 home runs. His blast in the 11th inning of the American League Championship Series opener would have been the game-winner had Oakland not responded with two runs to snatch victory from the jaws of defeat.

By 1974 Kaline had been relegated to full-time designated hitter. He believed he had achieved all he could—on September 24 of that season he reached the 3,000-hit milestone with a double off tough Dave McNally in Kaline's hometown of Baltimore. A week later a crowd of less than 5,000 trickled into Tiger Stadium to watch Kaline play his last major-league game and perhaps hit his 400th career home run. The temperature dropped to 36 degrees and a cold, blustery wind blew through the ballpark. And after going hitless in his first two at-bats he was done. "I've had it," he told manager Ralph Houk.[4] Had Kaline indeed smashed one over the fence, he would have been the first in American League history to reach 400 home runs and 3,000 hits. Boston superstar Carl Yastrzemski achieved that feat instead in 1979.

Kaline called the choice he made in leaving his last game his biggest regret as a ballplayer. "It was one of the worst, if not the worst, decisions I've ever made in my life," he admitted years later.[5] But the mistake after he announced his retirement on that day could not weaken the love Detroit fans have felt for him ever since.

In 1976, four years before his inevitable induction into the Baseball Hall of Fame, Kaline launched his career as a color commentator on Tigers television broadcasts. He remained in that role for a quarter-century, barely longer than his playing career. His capacity with the club extended beyond announcing. Kaline served as a spring training instructor, then special advisor to owner Mike Ilitch in 2003 after leaving the booth.

The result of that continued association was more than 50 years affiliated with Detroit baseball. It is no wonder that he will forever be known affectionately as Mr. Tiger.

CHAPTER FIFTEEN

From Great to Average to Lousy

THE OLD "IF IT AIN'T BROKE DON'T FIX IT" PHILOSOPHY EMBRACED BY the Tigers heading into the 1969 season seemed appropriate. The defending world champions boasted an excellent mix of youth heading into their prime and still-viable 30-somethings who continued to perform well that year.

That mounds were lowered in every ballpark to bolster offense had little bearing on win totals—every team continued to compete on an even playing field. The earned run average of Detroit pitchers rose along with those of their peers on other clubs. And aside from second baseman Dick McAuliffe losing half his season to a knee injury, the Tigers remained relatively healthy throughout 1969.

Yet two major problems contributed to their inability to match their success of the previous year. One was pitcher Joe Sparma, whose poor control became so pronounced that he was removed from the rotation. Sparma struggled to focus and had lost the trust of manager Mayo Smith, whom he later claimed had no idea how to assemble a pitching staff. Sparma compiled a 6-8 record and poor 4.76 earned run average that year, then got dispatched to the expansion Montreal Expos. His career ended by age 29.

The other roadblock to a pennant was managed by Earl Weaver and featured one of the greatest rotations in baseball history. The Orioles won 109 games in 1969 (when the two-division setup was launched) and continued to dominate the American League East through 1971. Among their slew of premier starters was right-hander Pat Dobson, a decent reliever for Detroit until he was traded to San Diego for Joe Niekro, who continued his own mediocrity in 1970 and beyond until he discovered the knuckleball years later and emerged as a standout. Dobson was among three 20-game winners for Baltimore in 1971 and continued to pitch well for several years.

The Birds proved so dominant from the start that the Tigers fell further back in the standings despite a 23-9 run in April and May. A pitching collapse the next season dropped them under .500 for the first time since 1963. The primary culprit was McLain, who fell apart on and off the mound.

The downfall of perhaps the most bizarre player in franchise history began with a *Sports Illustrated* article published in February 1970. It claimed the foot injury that forced him to miss six starts down the stretch of the 1967 pennant race resulted from a gang-related stomping motivated by his failure to pay off gambling debts. McLain had established a bookmaking operation out of a Flint restaurant from which one of his bookies failed to pay off $43,000 in losses. A gangster threatened McLain, then broke his foot.

Denny McLain was among the premier pitchers in the sport until his personal demons dragged him down.
COURTESY OF THE NATIONAL BASEBALL HALL OF FAME LIBRARY

The *SI* story further contended that the same thug had placed bets on the Red Sox and Twins to win the pennant that year and also put money down on the Angels to beat the Tigers on the last day of the season in a game McLain pitched. McLain was pounded in the start, and the Sox indeed captured the AL crown that afternoon because of it. McLain denied the allegations, telling MLB commissioner Bowie Kuhn that he had indeed invested $15,000 in a bookmaking operation but had ditched it before the race heated up in 1967.

No explanation could placate Kuhn, who suspended McLain for the first three months of the 1970 season. A throng of 53,863 filled Tiger Stadium for his return on July 1. Little did anyone in the crowd realize that it marked the beginning of the end for McLain, who would never recapture the magic that once kept the best hitters off-balance at the plate. He was clobbered by the Yankees that night and finished the season with a 3-5 record and 4.63 ERA.

His troubles had scarcely begun. He behaved erratically. The club suspended him for dumping ice water on two sportswriters. He was later barred from playing yet again, this time for the remainder of the season, for carrying a gun on a team flight. Soon he declared bankruptcy, claiming debts of $446,069.

Tigers GM Jim Campbell then caught a break. He found a patsy in Senators owner Bob Short, who knew little about baseball and displayed a greater motivation for making a splash than winning ballgames before moving the club to Texas in 1972. Short became fascinated with McLain. So two days before the 1970 World Series he sent promising young third baseman Aurelio Rodríguez, slick-fielding shortstop Eddie Brinkman, and ace right-hander Joe Coleman for McLain, aging infielder Don Wert, and part-time outfielder Elliott Maddox.

It was grand larceny, and Senators manager Ted Williams knew it. "This was not my trade. It looks now that we gave up more than we should," he said while placing his nomination for the Understatement of the Year Award.[1]

As the Tigers suspected, McLain continued his downward spiral after arriving in Washington. He undermined Williams, even forming a secret society among his teammates that served that purpose. He also performed horribly, complaining about pitching on four days' rest instead of three, and compiled a 10-22 record in 1971.

Meanwhile, the newcomers contributed quite nicely to the Tigers. But a newcomer who arrived six days later made the biggest impact. And that was fiery manager Billy Martin, who before and after his stint in Detroit boasted a penchant for turning losers into winners, then losing job after job because of his combative nature with players, umpires, and management, which was exacerbated by alcoholism.

Beat writer Jim Hawkins reported years later that the Twins warned the Tigers against hiring Martin. But the advice was ignored. "The players were tired of Mayo Smith and quit on him, so the front office was desperate," Hawkins said. "Billy had a reputation as a good manager with veterans so they thought they could squeeze one more championship out of the aging veterans like Al Kaline, Norm Cash, Willie Horton, Bill Freehan, Mickey Lolich and Dick McAuliffe."[2]

Martin had come close in his only season in Minnesota, which won a division title before losing the pennant to Baltimore. But he punched his way out of that job by socking Twins soon-to-be-20-game-winner Dave Boswell repeatedly in an alley outside the Lindell AC bar in Detroit in August 1969. The blow resulted in the pitcher requiring 20 stitches in his face. Boswell missed several starts in the midst of a pennant race after the pummeling, which left him unconscious. So Martin was fired after that season.

The new manager received a wonderful gift in the trade that provided him with a new left side of the infield and co-ace to go along with Lolich. Martin rode his team hard, as he typically did throughout his stormy career. He pitched Lolich more than every fourth day in a futile effort to catch the powerful Orioles. The left-hander made a ridiculous 45 starts and pitched 376 innings, nearly 100 more than he had ever previously worked in a season. He and Coleman combined for 45 wins as the newcomer also recorded a career-high in innings pitched.

Martin believed such was required because his club boasted little pitching depth in 1971 and ranked eighth in the American League in team ERA. But he refused to back down even after the Tigers had fallen hopelessly out of the race by mid-August. Lolich pitched complete games in 15 of his last 17 starts.

So eager were the Tigers to win one more crown that Campbell signed two games into the season an old friend of Martin's—none other than Dave Boswell. Martin planted him on the bullpen bench, where he pretty much remained for nearly two months before his release. Boswell pitched a mere 4⅓ innings over three relief outings for Detroit.

Martin was a mystery. He was motivational despite his abrasiveness. Some players hated him (including Northrup, who called him the worst manager he ever played for) and others loved him. In the modern era under another manager, Lolich likely would have thrown about half that many innings. But he embraced the workload Martin forced upon him. He had been told by the new manager upon his arrival that he would remain on the mound no matter the circumstances, and Martin was true to his word. Lolich recalled one game during which he was getting battered early and gazed to the bullpen to see if anyone was warming up.

"I then glanced at him standing on the dugout steps with his arms folded staring at me," Lolich said. "I got out of the inning and when I walked into the dugout he said, 'Who the F were you looking at?' I said, 'I was kind of getting shelled and thought you might make a move.' He said, 'don't you remember, I said that you are in the game until at least the sixth no matter what the score is?' I then shut out the Orioles the rest of the way. Billy lived by those rules and he gave me a load of confidence. I liked the guy and he made all the difference for me in my career. He was the best manager I ever played for. He knew what was going on and was always two innings ahead of the other manager."[3]

What Martin needed in 1972 was the Orioles to fly back down to earth and for his aging position players (only one who recorded at least 100 at-bats opened the season younger than 29 years old) to maintain their productivity. The Birds indeed descended to mediocrity, causing a logjam atop the Eastern Division. The Tigers performed no better as a team than they had in 1971—not one hitter managed more than 62 RBIs—but they took advantage of the poor competition to wage a battle with Boston for the crown.

They remained in first or second place from late April forward and spent most of the season atop the standings. Campbell pulled off an astute move in early August by signing veteran starting pitcher Woodie Fryman, who had been dispatched by the pathetic Phillies. The southpaw, who had made the successful transition from power pitcher to control pitcher, performed brilliantly from the moment he donned a Detroit uniform. He hurled 18⅔ shutout innings that included a complete-game blanking of New York in Yankee Stadium. Fryman won 10 of 13 decisions and compiled a sparkling 2.03 ERA down the stretch. His craftiness on the mound frustrated the hitters of his day. "Trying to hit Woodie Fryman is like trying to eat soup with a fork," offered former teammate Larry Bowa.[4]

His last victory clinched the title. Fryman had beaten Milwaukee three days earlier to launch a three-game sweep that set up a showdown series at Tiger Stadium against the Red Sox. Lolich vaulted the club into first place by striking out 15 in a 4–1 victory that featured home runs by Kaline and Rodríguez. Fryman doomed Boston the next night before a second consecutive crowd of more than 50,000 with a 3–1 win in which he outpitched legend Luis Tiant.

The mountain required to climb for a shot at the World Series seemed too steep. The Western Division champion Athletics were younger, far more athletic, and simply better in all areas of the game. They boasted more power and speed, as well as greater pitching depth. So when they won the first two games in Oakland many believed the Tigers were destined to be swept. Martin and his players lost their cool in Game 2 after Oakland veteran Bert Campaneris fired his bat at pitcher Lerrin LaGrow after a hit-by-pitch. The manager had to be restrained from attacking Campaneris.

The Tigers refused to die. Coleman pitched a shutout in Game 3, then Lolich performed brilliantly through nine innings the next day to keep his team alive. Detroit appeared to be cooked yet again when Oakland scored twice in the 10th inning against relief ace and one-year wonder Chuck Seelbach. But singles by McAuliffe, Kaline, and Northrup, the last a game-winner, sent the series back to Oakland for the clincher.

Fryman and Athletics starter John "Blue Moon" Odom rose to the occasion. A critical McAuliffe error in the fourth inning led to a run that gave the Athletics a 2–1 lead. While Fryman mowed through the rugged lineup thereafter, Odom and young rotation mate Vida Blue did the same against Detroit, which could not get a runner past first base the rest of the way. So much for a pennant celebration.

The Tigers were losing a race against Father Time. A rebuild was inevitable, and Martin was not the ideal manager for that. Every extensively used position player and starting pitcher aside from Rodríguez and Coleman opened the 1973 season at age 30 or older. Even relative newcomers such as slugger Frank Howard, Duke Sims, and Tony Taylor had reached the end of their careers.

Brilliant seasons from Coleman, who won a career-high 23 games, and closer John Hiller, who led the league with 38 saves, prevented a complete collapse. But a 5-13 slide in late August and two more outbursts by Martin—one before and one after—resulted in a change at the helm.

The first meltdown was directed at Campbell late in spring training. The general manager had increased a fine Martin levied against Horton, who had emotionally checked out since being informed by the manager that he would no longer be a lineup regular and even told the media he would not work as hard. Martin bolted the club. "I'm done. Get yourself a new manager," he told Campbell before leaving. Martin then returned the next day with an explanation for reporters. "I was just upset and said the hell with it," he said. "I had no intention of quitting. I'll be honest with you. I don't even remember saying anything about quitting. Maybe I said it, but I don't remember. I had to get away for a day. Maybe I got mad at something when I should have sat there a little longer and talked things out."[5]

Campbell let it slide with the understanding that the feisty Martin tended to allow his emotions to dictate his actions. And all was well until the Tigers started losing. The last three of those defeats came at home against lowly Cleveland. His anger piqued when he watched Indians ace Gaylord Perry mow down his hitters by throwing what the Hall of Famer later admitted was a spitball, Martin ordered Coleman and fellow Tigers pitcher Fred Scherman to use saliva and Vaseline on their pitches, then confirmed his edict to the media. That admission resulted in a suspension from American League president Joe Cronin and, inevitably, his firing by Campbell. Martin was replaced by coach Joe Schultz, whose lone claim to fame was managing the 1969 Seattle Pilots in their only season of existence and being quoted as repeating his made-up word "shitfuck" in the controversial Jim Bouton book *Ball Four*.

New skipper Ralph Houk was about to lead a group far less talented than the Yankees of the early 1960s that he guided to three pennants and two World Series titles. The 1974 and 1975 clubs featured veteran hitters hanging on to their careers for dear life and fading pitchers, including Coleman, who at age 27 had already begun his descent. His ERA skyrocketed nearly two points over those two years as he lost control. Coleman walked 93 batters in 1973 and 158 the following year. He zeroed back in on the strike zone in 1975, but hitters zeroed in on his pitches and banged them all over AL ballparks.

"I've never seen a pitcher at his age, who never has had any arm problems have as much trouble as Joe has had for us the last two years," Houk claimed in wonderment.[6] But interviewed years later, Coleman begged to differ. He complained about a shoulder issue, though he also admitted a sense of frustration. "At times, I didn't have any idea what I was doing out there," he said.[7]

Neither did his rotation mates. Lolich lost 21 games and posted his worst ERA in eight years in 1974; he left after the next season for the Mets in a wise trade for slugger Rusty Staub. And LaGrow, a prized prospect, never found his groove as a starter. He was swapped to St. Louis and eventually hit his stride for two years as a closer for the White Sox.

The result was that the Tigers went from boasting one of the premier pitching staffs in the American League to suffering with the worst. They ranked last in team ERA in 1974 and 11th in 1975, when the club bottomed out under Houk. Its 57-102 record was its worst since 1952. Only Horton, Freehan, and Stanley remained among the everyday players who helped bring a world championship to Detroit in 1968 and division crown four years later.

Attendance had dropped nearly 700,000 since 1973. The Tigers were not about to regain their dominance. But they needed a shot in the arm in 1976, a reason for fans to come to the ballpark. They did not receive one booster shot. They received two. One was a gangly kid who talked to baseballs on the mound, and the other emerged from a prison cell to take the sport by storm.

CHAPTER SIXTEEN

The Base Thief and The Bird

IT HAS BEEN OFFERED AS PRAISE FOR MAJOR LEAGUE BASEBALL THAT IT brings together as a family people from all walks of life. Usually more for better than for worse, young men of various nationalities and backgrounds become teammates. One striking example of that diversity spotlighted the two most impactful players on the 1976 Tigers. They were African-American outfielder Ron LeFlore and white pitcher Mark "The Bird" Fidrych.

The two blossomed that season though LeFlore first donned a Detroit uniform two years earlier. The remarkability of his achievement cannot be overstated given his upbringing in the crime-infested east side. His father had lost his job with one of the many car manufacturers in the Motor City and tried to find solace in a bottle. His son soon fell victim to addiction to heroin while turning to crime to fund his drug habit. He dropped out of school and committed a series of thefts, including an armed robbery at a Detroit bar that landed him in prison at the tender age of 15 in 1963.

His sentence was 5 to 15 years. But it was time well spent, because not only did it provide structure to his life, it also gave him the opportunity to play baseball for the first time. He proved himself to be a natural. Tigers manager Billy Martin learned through a fellow inmate about his talent. A visit to the prison confirmed that LeFlore boasted potential. Martin arranged for a one-day parole so that he could try out in front of Tiger scouts and front office personnel, who were impressed by his blazing speed and ability to make consistent hard contact with the bat. They arranged to sign him to a minor-league contract after he had completed his sentence. The Tigers had benefited years earlier from giving an ex-con a tryout when they signed super pinch-hitter Gates Brown.

LeFlore quickly emerged as a phenom. After a short stint with Class A Clinton, he was eventually promoted to Triple-A and finally Detroit in 1974. He adjusted well enough to major-league pitching to bat .260 and steal 23 bases. After stagnating a bit as the starting center fielder the following year, he blossomed in 1976.

But LeFlore flourished in the shadow of Fidrych, whose background differed greatly. The latter grew up in a middle-class family in the small Massachusetts town of Northboro, the son of an assistant high school principal. His unpretentious "boy next door" personality remained with

Ron LeFlore went from prison to stardom for the Tigers in the 1970s.
COURTESY OF THE NATIONAL BASEBALL HALL OF FAME LIBRARY

him throughout his life and emerged as the driving force behind the love Detroit fans and all of America felt for him.

Perhaps one reason for his humbleness was that he never starred as an amateur. He played all three major sports in high school but received no college scholarship offers. Scouts never flocked to see him pitch, but he did pique the interest of the Red Sox and Tigers. Impressed with his fastball velocity, Detroit bird dog Joe Cusick recommended he be drafted, and he was indeed snagged in the 10th round in 1974.

The gangly blond kid with the curly mop-top hairstyle who weighed just 175 pounds despite a height of 6-foot-3 was nicknamed "Big Bird" (from *Sesame Street* fame) by coach Joe Hogan at Class A Bristol. But that moniker would have died in obscurity had Fidrych not justified Cusick's faith in him. He skyrocketed through the system as a starter, earning three promotions in 1975 after winning all three decisions and fanning 40 in just 34 innings the previous season as a reliever. His performance improved at every level. Fidrych compiled a 4-1 mark with a 1.58 ERA at Triple-A Evansville and displayed the pinpoint control that had eluded him earlier.

Eccentric right-hander Mark Fidrych gained wild popularity throughout the country in 1976 before fading.
COURTESY OF DREAMSTIME, COPYRIGHT JERRY COLI

A five-game losing streak that began a 3-12 stretch in May sent the Tigers reeling out of the pennant race permanently. Such was not unexpected after their 104-loss season in 1975. Yet the eyes of the baseball world were rigidly fixed on Detroit, where LeFlore and Fidrych earned attention.

LeFlore emerged as the hottest hitter in the sport. Nobody expected when he opened an April 17 game against the host Angels with a double that it would launch a 30-game hitting streak, which remained through 2021 the longest in franchise history by any player not named Ty Cobb (who hit safely in 40 straight games in 1911). LeFlore took advantage of the leadoff spot that maximized at-bats. He finished his remarkable run batting .392 after raising his average to .409 in late May. Weak hitting behind him often prevented the Tigers from scoring LeFlore, who stole 12 bases during his tear, including four in one game against the White Sox.

By that time, however, Fidrych had stolen the spotlight, not simply by mowing down the opposition. His quirky actions on the mound inspired curiosity not just in Detroit but throughout the country. He spurred interest in a team that had been losing fans by talking to himself and to the baseball before delivering pitches, dropping to his hands and knees to smooth out the dirt, strutting nervously around like, well, a big bird, between batters, and thanking teammates and even umpires for a job well done before what became an inevitable curtain call demanded by Tiger fans after victories. "I talked to older guys who knew the Babe Ruth era and they said there was more excitement that summer than ever because Fid brought fun back to the game," recalled former teammate John Wockenfuss.[1]

The eccentricities of Fidrych might not have gone unnoticed but certainly would not have been embraced had he not performed brilliantly. He consistently pitched down in the strike zone. His lively slider featured late movement resulting in one groundout after another. Detroit defenders loved playing behind him because he worked fast and frequently forced weak contact. The beloved rookie opened the season in the bullpen, hurled a complete-game two-hitter against Cleveland in his first start, then rose to greatness and fame. He won eight consecutive outings from late May to early July, including seven complete games and one shutout. The streak was broken in a 1–0 loss to Kansas City, which was followed by an 11-inning Fidrych blanking of Oakland.

He reached the height of his national popularity with a nationally televised start on *Monday Night Baseball* with the Yankees in town on June 28. A throng of nearly 50,000—unheard of on a weeknight—clicked through the turnstiles to watch their hero mow down the Bronx Bombers in a 5–1 victory. Game broadcaster John Prince could hardly contain himself. "He's giving me duck bumps and I've watched over 8,000 games," Prince proclaimed. "He's some kind of unbelievable."[2] Fidrych emerged from the dugout for a curtain call after it was over as the fans screamed their approval.

Teammate Rusty Staub spoke about the authenticity of his teammate after the victory. "It's no act," he said. "There's nothing contrived about him and that's what makes him a beautiful person. . . . There's an electricity that he brings out in everyone, the players and the fans. He's different. He's a 21-year-old kid with a great enthusiasm that everyone loves. He has an inner youth, an exuberance."[3]

Attendance skyrocketed in ballparks for games Fidrych was scheduled to pitch. The Tigers averaged 18,338 fans per game in 1976, but that figure was nearly doubled for those Fidrych pitched. Yet he remained unchanged—just an unassuming kid from a small Massachusetts town.

"He was the same guy I met as a non-roster invitee in spring training as he was all through the season," Tigers closer John Hiller said. "I was so impressed with everything he did, how he handled himself, his work ethic and how he had time for everyone. He was so great with the fans."

Neither 1976 standout enjoyed happy endings with the Tigers. But while arm problems were derailing Fidrych's career, LeFlore continued to hit for a high average and run. He earned Tiger of the Year honors in 1977 by batting .325 before going on a stolen-base spree, leading the league with 68 (and 126 runs scored) in 1978 and adding 78 the next season. His performance and story were so remarkable that a movie about his life titled *One in a Million* featuring *Roots* star LeVar Burton was produced.

The feel-good story did not continue. LeFlore fell back into drug abuse and allowed an unsavory entourage to hang out in the clubhouse, angering new manager Sparky Anderson. The result was a trade to Montreal, with whom he stole 97 bases in 1980. He wore out his welcome there as well and was out of baseball two years later after his release from the White Sox due to drug and gun possession charges.

LeFlore felt hurt by perceived ill treatment by Tiger management. He spoke angrily about the club upon his departure. "(Alan) Trammell was there three years," he complained. "I was there five years. I had good stats every year. They paid Trammell [$2.8 million in a seven-year deal]. But they didn't feel it was necessary to pay me any more money."[4]

Years later he admitted that his troubled and turbulent past still negatively affected him during his career. And that left him bitter. "I really needed guidance and I didn't get that," he said. "How come I couldn't have gotten that guidance when I first came up? But I just didn't have the guidance that I should have had. I had no support from anybody. I don't know if they were afraid because I was an ex-inmate but nobody ever went out of their way to really help me. And I needed somebody. I really did. I really needed some help and some guidance, considering where I came from. And I didn't get it.

"Just think if I had played baseball as a kid instead of running the streets. Just think if I had improved my baseball skills instead of going to prison. How good could I have been? Who knows, if I had gotten that guidance that I needed, if I had known what was going on in society, I could have had some Hall of Fame stats."[5]

Perhaps Fidrych would boast a bust in Cooperstown had he not been victimized by bad luck. The beginning of the end occurred when he injured his knee shagging balls in spring training 1977. He returned in late May and won six straight decisions after two defeats—complete games one and all to lower his ERA to 1.83. But he was battered in his next two starts and removed in the first inning in a July 12 game against the expansion Toronto Blue Jays with an arm injury from which he never recovered.

Yet Fidrych never changed. He was not one to become bitter. Future World Series champion manager Jim Leyland, who later guided the

Tigers to two pennants, recalled how Fidrych remained the same friendly sort he had always been after his last start at Triple-A Evansville in 1980 before one final fling with the Tigers. "Mark was such a great kid and we tried everything we could to get him back to the big leagues," Leyland said. "Even in the minors he would fill stadiums because everyone wanted to see him. The day he got called up [to Detroit] he walked into our locker room with grease all over him because he changed the oil in our catcher's car. After he pitched that night he went around and shook everyone's hand."

Fidrych was out of baseball by 1983 after a stint in the Boston organization during which he failed to land a spot on the Red Sox roster. By that time the Tigers were a far cry from the lousy team they had been when The Bird was winning 19 games and the Rookie of the Year award while finishing second in the Cy Young balloting to Baltimore ace Jim Palmer. A youth movement had transformed them into a winner and, for one glorious season, the most dominant club in baseball.

CHAPTER SEVENTEEN

The Kids and a Spark from Sparky

IT IS CALLED FORCE-FEEDING AND IT CAN BE DANGEROUS. IT IS THE practice of allowing kids with little minor-league experience to sink or swim in the big leagues. The Tigers embraced that philosophy in the late 1970s. And it worked. Force-feeding allowed the organization not just to survive but to thrive despite the demise of Mark Fidrych and eventually the trade of Ron LeFlore.

They arrived in waves. First baseman Jason Thompson and pitcher Jack Morris in 1976. Outfielder Steve Kemp and pitcher Dave Rozema in 1977. Second baseman Lou Whitaker, shortstop Alan Trammell, and catcher Lance Parrish in 1978. Pitcher Dan Petry in 1979. One and all first donned a Detroit uniform no older than 22. One and all rocketed through the farm system. And one and all made positive impacts, some immediately.

The power-hitting Thompson wasted little time establishing himself. He landed in the Motor City less than a year after the Tigers snagged him in the fourth round of the 1975 amateur draft. By 1977 he was leading the club with 31 home runs and 105 RBIs and earning a spot on the American League All-Star team. Though a poor trade for outfielder Al Cowens sent Thompson to Seattle in 1980, he had played a significant role in the team's resurgence with his penchant for getting on base and driving in runs.

Morris made a far greater impact after pitching in just 32 minor-league games. His Hall of Fame career began in earnest in 1979 when he posted a 17-7 record and 3.28 ERA while displaying the intensity and competitiveness that marked his career, nearly all of which he spent with the Tigers despite notable stints with Minnesota and Toronto.

After compiling a .328 average in his only minor-league season, Kemp earned the distinction as one of the best first-year players in baseball history not to earn any Rookie of the Year votes. He smoked line drives all over the field, ranking third on the team in doubles with 29 and RBIs with 88. Like Thompson he emerged as a patient hitter who worked his walks while averaging 93 RBIs over his first four seasons.

The slow-throwing Rozema also made an immediate impact before losing his changeup and his effectiveness. He emerged immediately as the ace of the 1977 staff devastated by the Fidrych injury. His unimpres-

Tough Jack Morris sported a winning record in each of his first 10 seasons in Detroit.

COURTESY OF DREAMSTIME, COPYRIGHT JERRY COLI

sive 85-mile-an-hour fastball belied his large frame, but his penchant for throwing low strikes and keeping hitters off-balance resulted in a 15-7 record and 3.09 ERA as a rookie. A lack of run support and eventual move to the bullpen prevented him from reaching double figures in wins again, but he certainly impressed the competition his first season. Included were Indians manager Frank Robinson, who claimed Rozema boasted the potential to win 30 games, and Twins slugger Lyman Bostock, who complained that "the ball doesn't go anywhere" even when he made good contact on the changeup.[1]

The heart of the Tigers team that blossomed into a champion arrived in 1978. The most important defensive component of any club is strength up the middle, and three rookies established themselves in those positions that year. The first to arrive was Trammell, who after earning a cup of coffee in The Show the previous season placed fourth in the Rookie of the Year balloting in 1978 with steady fielding that would earn him four Gold Gloves. He eventually blossomed into an all-around player with power.

So did Whitaker, who beat out his infield mate for Rookie of the Year honors by batting .285. He became one of the most consistently productive offensive players in Tigers history and displayed the defensive talent from the start that would result in three consecutive Gold Glove awards. The Whitaker-Trammell combination remained in place for nearly two decades as one of the premier double-play duos in baseball history.

It took longer to navigate the path from the minors to the majors for Parrish, who was drafted in the first round out of high school. The tough 210-pounder was the ideal size for a catcher, and he too won three Gold Gloves. But the bonus was a potent bat that produced both average and power. Parrish proved himself one of the premier catchers in the sport at his peak from 1982 to 1986, averaging 28 home runs and 99 RBIs per season.

The final piece to the puzzle was Petry. After joining the rotation at age 20, he teamed with Morris to provide a tremendous one-two pitching punch with remarkable consistency. The right-hander compiled an 87-59 record from 1980 to 1985 while posting an under-4.00 ERA in each of those years before elbow problems wrecked his career.

Lance Parrish emerged as one of the top catchers in the sport in the early 1980s.
COURTESY OF DREAMSTIME, COPYRIGHT JERRY COLI

The immediate impact of all those players prevented the Tigers from feeling the effects of typical rebuilds. But in the powerful American League East, good was not good enough. They finished a mere fifth in 1978 and 1979 despite approaching 90 wins both seasons and continued to lag behind. The Yankees and Orioles steamrolled to championships in that era, the Red Sox remained strong, and even the once lowly Milwaukee Brewers bashed their way to a pennant in 1982.

The Tigers had gained respectability under manager Ralph Houk. But he considered that and calming the clubhouse after the Billy Martin era his primary goals, so having achieved them he rode off into the sunset, announcing his retirement a week before the end of the 1978 season. The 59-year-old, who returned three years later to manage the Red Sox, figured he had earned it and simply yearned to relax. "The time has come for me to go fishing and live a little bit," he said. "I feel good about leaving, though, because I feel good about the ball club. It's a good ball club now, and that wasn't the case when I came here."[2]

Houk was replaced by Triple-A manager Les Moss, who was not long for the job despite having become familiar with all the young standouts as they took their last step through the minor-league system. Even a hot stretch in late May could not save him with Sparky Anderson available. The man who drove the Big Red Machine to two World Series championships proved too appealing to bypass. Jim Campbell understood that both the players and fans would be sparked by Sparky far more than they had been by Moss, whose hiring had been criticized as uninspired. And with rumors flying that the Cubs were also interested, Campbell knew he had to act fast or face regret.

Anderson claimed at first he was unavailable until 1980. Campbell expressed a sense of guilt over the possibility of using Moss as a lame-duck manager all year. Anderson warned him that he would not come cheaply, but Campbell was game. He believed his team was ready to blossom into a champion, and he would spare little expense to hire a proven champion. So he fired Moss and signed Anderson to a five-year contract.

The new manager was ebullient at his introductory press conference. He had always embraced opportunities to work with talented young players, and the Tigers boasted plenty of them. He predicted his team would win a World Series crown within five years—and nailed it.

Anderson preached discipline and what he perceived as maturity. He demanded his players wear a coat and tie on the road and shave off all facial hair (though he eventually backed off on the latter order). Morris recalled the first meeting Anderson had with his team. "He was very blunt and let everyone know who was in control by saying 'it's either my way or the highway and we're going to weed out the rats.'"[3]

The positive effects of the Anderson hire were far from immediate. The Tigers lost 9 of 11 upon his arrival, greatly due to the struggles of John Hiller, who was fading fast and was in the process of losing the closer role to Aurelio López. The team continued to hang around .500 before catching fire in mid-August. A 14-3 run ensured a winning record, but some wondered if Moss could have performed just as well.

That concern proved legitimate through 1982 as the Tigers remained on the outside looking in at the pennant race year after year while barely achieving winning records. Adding to the worries about the direction of the club were the tweaks that weakened the lineup. The power-hitting Thompson was traded in May 1980 for Cowens, who failed to live up to offensive expectations. Thompson was replaced at first base by former Pirate standout Richie Hebner, who exploded in 1980 with 82 RBIs before fading and getting shipped back to Pittsburgh. Fellow run producer Kemp was dispatched to the White Sox for center fielder Chet Lemon, who emerged as a Tiger mainstay but only in 1984 found the batting stroke that made him a consistent .300 hitter in Chicago.

The result of that tinkering was that Detroit descended from the premier offensive club in the American League in 1980 to a mediocre one by 1982. Only a steal of a deal that brought power-hitting outfielder Larry Herndon to Detroit prevented a greater disaster. A strong rotation featuring Morris, Petry, and steady 1977 acquisition Milt Wilcox was being wasted by poor run support and relievers who all too often turned victory into defeat.

No additions in 1983 promised a resurgence. The Tigers needed their still-young stars to blossom. And that appeared quite unlikely when they opened the season at 17-22 while falling six games out of first place. Then suddenly they started to sizzle. A four-game sweep of the Red Sox at Fenway Park and 18-5 blitz thrust the Tigers into second place, just 1½ games off the pace. They won 15 of 21 during one stretch in July and remained a mere 1 game out of first place despite an August slump. The torrid Orioles eventually pulled away, but the Tigers proved themselves a contender heading into 1984.

The heart of the lineup and rotation had reached their prime. And the emergence of an all-around talent and inspirational outfielder, as well as the acquisition of a lights-out closer, were about to catapult the Tigers to greatness.

CHAPTER EIGHTEEN

Wire to Wire

THE BASEBALL WORLD BARELY BLINKED AN EYE A WEEK BEFORE THE 1984 regular season when the Tigers made what seemed to be just a moderately important trade engineered by new general manager Bill Lajoie, a former scouting director and assistant to Campbell who had taken over the reins. He sent outfielder Glenn Wilson to Philadelphia for 29-year-old reliever Willie Hernández.

Neither player had set the sport on fire. Wilson was moved to make room in the lineup for aging slugger Darrell Evans. But manager Sparky Anderson planned for the swap to make a tremendous impact. He not only needed to strengthen his bullpen but also yearned to move promising second-year slugger Kirk Gibson from DH to right field.

Bingo.

One could not have imagined the positive effect that one swap would have on the Tigers. Hernández had spent the previous seven seasons as a decent reliever with average stuff. He annually allowed about a hit per inning and banked on good control to remain effective. Before the 1984 season he began working on what was then a new pitch. It was the cut fastball, which sliced into right-handed hitters while his screwball moved away. The devastating differences between those two pitches combined with a fine curveball gave Hernández a deadly repertoire. The cut fastball forced weak contact. The other deliveries kept batters guessing and off-balance.

The effects were mind-blowing. Hernández quickly earned co-closer status with Aurelio López, though neither pitched in many save situations while the Tigers destroyed foe after foe. Both registered seven saves through May. But so dominant had Hernández become that he was quietly ordained the primary closer by early June. His workload grew immensely—this was not yet the era in which closers were called upon almost exclusively for one-inning stints. Hernández recorded four saves in four appearances in early June that required him to pitch more than nine total innings. During one stretch he surrendered a mere three earned runs in 37⅓ innings to lower his ERA to 1.94.

Meanwhile. Gibson emerged as a triple offensive threat and an extra-base-hit machine. He slammed 27 home runs and even 10 triples while displaying his speed and daring on the basepaths with 29 steals. But the brash outfielder clashed with his old-school manager. Anderson considered Gibson conceited and self-centered. That lack of professionalism motivated Anderson to keep the standout sitting on the bench against left-handers, never mind that Gibson batted .366 versus southpaws in 1981. The intense Gibson flew into a rage when Anderson announced on Opening Day 1983 that he would remain a platoon player and designated hitter. A confrontation in Anderson's office ended with the manager telling him to "open the door and get your ass outta here."[1]

Gibson got his ass out of there but not in gear at the plate. He slumped so badly his average dropped to .164 in mid-May. He then lost two weeks to minor knee surgery before embarking on a tear during which he showed off his power with a 523-foot blast over the right field roof at Tiger Stadium and his speed with an inside-the-park home run in the same game. Offered legendary baseball writer Peter Gammons in a *Sporting News* article, "He is as much fun to watch as any player in this league, whether hitting 523-foot home runs, racing out of control around the bases, or just plain running. Unlike some of the supposedly exciting base-running types, he is worth the price of admission every time he goes into motion."[2]

Anderson remained critical, especially after Gibson slumped again, losing his batting stroke and falling to .227 while Tiger fans booed him constantly and the media turned against him. He was approaching 27 years old, and he finally understood that he would continue spinning his wheels unless he embraced an attitude change. "I lost my focus," he recalled years later. "I wasn't a good player. I had poor work habits."[3]

Sparky Anderson sparked the Tigers to the world title in 1984.
COURTESY OF DREAMSTIME, COPYRIGHT JERRY COLI

Not in 1984. Gibson spent four days before that season at the Pacific Institute in Seattle with mental adviser Frank Bartenetti, who taught him how to replace negative images in his mind with positive ones. Gibson also embarked on a tough workout regimen such as the one that helped make him a top wide receiver at Michigan State and draft pick by the NFL St. Louis Cardinals. He willingly worked in spring training with Tigers legend Al Kaline to sharpen his skills in right field. His new attitude motivated pitching coach Roger Craig to convince Anderson to make him an everyday player. Craig proved so persuasive that the club unloaded Wilson.

With the blossoming of Hernández and Gibson, the final parts of a machine had been put into place. The 1984 team became a steamroller with every component working at maximum power and efficiency. The Tigers were more like cheetahs out of the gate, sprinting from the start and pulling away from the pack. They swept Minnesota, Chicago, and Texas in starting the season 8-0. They won seven straight in late April. They swept Cleveland and Kansas City on the road. Then they hit the quarter pole with a 9-0 run against Seattle, Oakland, and California to raise their record to 35-5. The greatest start in major-league history placed Detroit 8½ games up on the blossoming Blue Jays in the AL East.

A minislump in late May and early June knocked five games off the lead. The Tigers played .500 baseball for six weeks but increased their advantage. Then the machine revved up its engines again. The rotation quartet of Morris, Petry, Wilcox, and Rozema heated up while the hitters clicked on all cylinders. The result was an 11-1 blitz that put the division title away by late July. The Tigers again traded victories and defeats as they cruised to the crown before ensuring they would enter the playoffs with momentum by winning 11 of 15 in late September.

The season-ending numbers were downright frightening. Not one Tiger scored or drove in 100 runs, yet they led the American League in runs. Not one starter won 20 games or recorded an ERA under 3.24, yet they registered the lowest ERA in the AL. Morris, Petry, and Wilcox combined for 54 victories. Hernández won nine games and saved 32 to run away with the Cy Young and even Most Valuable Player awards.

His contributions were barely required when the Tigers traveled to Kansas City for the ALCS. The starting trio rolled through a Royals lineup that featured superspeedy leadoff hitter Willie Wilson and Hall of Famer George Brett. Trammell tripled and homered to support Morris in a runaway Game 1 victory, then the Tigers overcame a rare hiccup by Hernández to take the second game when line-drive hitter Johnny Grubb slammed a two-run double in the 11th inning.

The Tigers returned home for a Friday afternoon showdown before a sellout crowd of 52,168, and Wilcox rose to the occasion by yielding just three hits before giving way to Hernández in a 1–0 victory that clinched their first pennant since 1968.

"This is the toughest group of guys I've ever seen," Gibson said as he and his teammates celebrated the triumph. "It's hard to explain . . . how much confidence and chemistry there is among all 25 guys. But this is a group of guys that fight in the pit better than any other athletic team I've ever been on."[4]

Sending a comparatively weak San Diego club to the World Series against a Tigers team playing at the top of their game was like sending a lamb to its slaughter. Those that believed the Padres had no chance were proven justified. Trammell and Gibson combined to hit more home runs and drive in nearly as many runs as did all their opponents combined. Folk hero Kurt Bevacqua provided the only highlight for the Padres with a three-run homer off Petry to win Game 2, but Wilcox and Morris shut them down when the series returned to Detroit. Then the Tigers overcame another poor start by Petry in Game 5 as Gibson bludgeoned San Diego with two home runs, including one off heat-throwing closer Goose Gossage, and Parrish added another. López and Hernández polished off the Padres to secure the 8–4 victory and World Series championship.

The blast against Gossage was sweet vindication for Gibson, who had struggled against him in the past. Anderson flashed four fingers to Gibson as he stepped in to indicate his belief that the Padres would walk him to set up a double play. "Ten bucks they pitch to me and I crank it," he yelled to his manager. They did—and he did deep into the right field bleachers.

"It's a beautiful ending to a beautiful season," said Gibson, who had also stolen a run when he raced home from third after a popup was caught by second baseman Alan Wiggins. "When the chips are down I always want to be the guy they count on."[5]

Many in Detroit soon wished they could have counted on the revelers celebrating peacefully. But what followed was among the most violent reactions to a sports championship in American history. Police hoping to maintain order were overwhelmed by thousands of fans who besieged the field. As some outside the ballpark, many of them drunk, rushed in to join the compatriots, others stormed out of Tiger Stadium to help start a riot. They overturned cars and set fires while those yearning to celebrate peacefully scurried for their own vehicles.

After receiving boos and catcalls, Detroit mayor Coleman Young praised the throng that poured downtown for the victory parade that snaked down Michigan Avenue by contrasting them with the hooligans. "What we see here today are the real Tiger fans," he said. "What we have here today is the greatest baseball team in the world."[6]

Though Anderson elicited some cheers for boldly predicting a title repeat in 1985, the most raucous reaction was saved for Gibson, who raised both arms and screamed as he hopped up and down on the stage.

And the manager's crystal ball proved quite faulty. The Tigers opened the next season 6-0 and hung around the division race for half a season before a 2-8 stretch sent them slip-sliding away. The club scored 100 fewer runs that season, greatly due to significant drops in production from Herndon and Lemon.

Pitching problems arose as well. A shoulder injury doomed Wilcox by June. Though starting pitcher Walt Terrell performed well that year and two seasons beyond, the trade that brought him from the Mets cost them emerging slugger Howard Johnson. And 32-year-old free agent newcomer Frank Tanana was forced to reinvent himself after losing the life on his fastball. Though he made the transition successfully, he remained a far cry from the southpaw stud that dominated hitters with the Angels a decade earlier.

The heart of the club featuring Morris, Parrish, Whitaker, Trammell, Gibson, and first baseman Darrell Evans, who like a fine wine seemed to improve with age, guaranteed that the Tigers remained strong in the years following their World Series victory. But the level of competition precluded any less than greatness earning crowns. Five of seven Eastern Division teams finished .500 or better in 1985 and 1986. The Tigers compiled an 87-75 record in the second of those seasons, yet never sniffed contention and finished closer to fifth place than first. And when they lost twice to Milwaukee in mid-June 1987 to drop 7½ games off the pace, another season of frustration appeared certain.

Then it happened. The Tigers got white-hot around Independence Day. A 17-5 run catapulted them to within a half-game of the lead. A three-game sweep of the visiting Twins that drew 116,000 fans vaulted Detroit atop the division. Meanwhile, Lajoie was working to ensure that his team would stay in contention by trading minor-league starting pitcher John Smoltz to Atlanta for 36-year-old right-hander Doyle Alexander in a swap that would result in short-term success and long-term disaster beyond anyone's wildest imagination.

Working for his ninth team as an inconsistent journeyman, Alexander had been performing poorly with the Braves in previous starts. He allowed four runs in six innings to Kansas City in a first outing with Detroit that certainly did not foretell the future. For suddenly Alexander began pitching like he had never pitched before. He hurled shutout ball in five of his next eight starts and won them all to conclude his 1987 stint following the trade with a 9-0 record and eyebrow-raising 1.53 ERA.

His last triumph was a 4-3 defeat of Toronto that pushed the Tigers into a first-place tie with the Blue Jays. A crowd of 45,026 at Tiger Stadium watched their team overtake Toronto when Trammell slammed a walkoff single in the 11th inning. Tanana required only a Herndon home run to polish off the Jays and clinch the division title with a 1–0 shutout the following day as 51,005 packed the ballpark. And as the Tigers celebrated, Whitaker grabbed second base, pulled it out of the ground, and later gave it to his double-play partner with the following inscription: "To Alan Trammell, MVP, 1987. Congratulations, Louis Rodman Whitaker."

Hall of Famer Alan Trammell was a marvel at the plate and at shortstop.
COURTESY OF DREAMSTIME,
COPYRIGHT SPORTS IMAGES

Trammell finished a close second to Jays slugger George Bell in the MVP voting, but only the former continued his season in the playoffs. The problem was Alexander could not maintain his excellence. He was clobbered by the Twins in Games 1 and 5 and had plenty of company among his rotation mates in his misery. Terrell, Morris, and Tanana were also victimized by Minnesota. The four starters allowed 25 earned runs in 28⅓ innings in recording all four losses.

It was the beginning of the end of an era. Just as the Tigers struggled when the core of their 1968 championship team aged, they did again when the group that snagged the 1984 championship got old, left in free agency, or was traded. Parrish bolted for Philadelphia before the 1987 season. Gibson signed with the Dodgers the following January. Evans was finally declining at age 41. Lemon faded as he approached his mid-30s. Even Trammell and Whitaker showed signs of slowing down as they hit their 30s, though both remained viable and even sometimes brilliant well into their next decade.

Lou Whitaker teamed with Alan Trammell to form a dynamite double-play combination in the 1980s.
COURTESY OF DREAMSTIME, COPYRIGHT JERRY COLI

The Tigers managed one more foray into contention in 1988 before a collapse from which they never fully recovered for two decades. They managed to hang around in the race despite their failure to replace Parrish and Gibson with viable offensive talent. New starting catcher Matt Nokes had displayed tremendous promise in 1987 by compiling 32 home runs and 87 RBIs to finish third in the Rookie of the Year voting, but his numbers plummeted and he was traded to the Yankees in 1990. Speedster Gary Pettis replaced Gibson in the outfield and proved far more effective defensively than offensively. Most damaging in the trade-off was the difference in power.

A rotation that included homegrown one-hit wonder Jeff Robinson, who went 13-6 with a 2.98 ERA and fine 1.12 WHIP (Walks and Hits per Inning Pitched), kept the Tigers alive through most of 1988. A 15-6 run to start June highlighted by a three-game home sweep of the Yankees vaulted them into first place. A torrid race raged involving five teams. They managed to stay mostly in front into early September despite several short slumps. But the last one was a doozy. They lost 13 of 15, including four straight at Tiger Stadium to fellow contender Milwaukee, to fall from their perch. Detroit went nearly four weeks without winning two straight. They went 9-3 down the stretch to chop their deficit from six games to one in a classic too-little-too-late scenario. Two defeats to the lowly Indians provided the knockout blow.

Given the pitching pieces destined to return in 1989, and despite inevitable offensive struggles, few could have predicted such a drastic downfall.

But through it all—aside from one season—a Hall of Fame broadcaster remained in the booth colorfully describing every victory, every defeat. And though many embraced ballplayers have donned Detroit uniforms over the years, nobody associated with the Tigers has ever been more beloved than the legendary Ernie Harwell.

Chapter Nineteen

"Like the House by the Side of the Road"

MOST RADIO ANNOUNCERS WHO HAVE DESCRIBED BASEBALL GAMES throughout history have felt as distant to the listener figuratively as they have physically. Though they likely painted a vivid picture of the action on the field, they made little emotional connection to those hearing their voices.

Then there was Ernie Harwell. For three generations he made friends with Tiger fans, most of whom he never met personally. He was seemingly talking baseball in their living rooms or sitting in the car seat next to them. That is how close he became through the force of his voice and personality from the moment he began broadcasting Detroit games in 1960. He achieved that distinction with ease and with clever phrases that made him unique and connected him to Tiger followers no matter their level of passion.

A called strikeout victim "stood there like the house by the side of the road and watched that one go by." Or he was "called out for excessive window shopping." Harwell cited any nearby town or suburb as the home of a lucky fan who snagged a foul ball. "A woman from Grosse Pointe caught that one," he told listeners. "It's loooooooong gone!" he shouted after a Tiger home run. "That's strike three. Mr. Rice said so," he stressed to the audience in citing an umpire's decision.[1]

His familiar southern drawl was a product of his upbringing in Atlanta, where his family moved after spending the first five years of his life in the tiny Georgia town of Washington. The son of a combination furniture store and funeral parlor owner, he embraced playing and

The great Ernie Harwell in 2006, four years before his death

listening to baseball when radio broadcasting of the sport was still in its infancy. He humored visitors at a local drugstore by imagining himself announcing games played by the minor-league Atlanta Crackers.

Harwell attended his first major-league contest while visiting a relative in Chicago at age 16 and that same year offered to serve as an Atlanta baseball correspondent for the *Sporting News*, which was accepted after editors grew impressed with his writing talent without knowing his age. He debuted on radio as a sports analyst as a senior at Emory University and soon landed a job as sports director at WSB in Atlanta, which eventually became home of the Braves. His opportunity to interview such baseball legends as Ty Cobb, Ted Williams, and Connie Mack offered invaluable experience.

Even his military duty during World War II provided a chance to hone his skills, as he toiled for a Marine newspaper and proved so impressive in a short stint broadcasting Crackers games for real that he landed the job permanently upon his discharge in 1946. His talent became immediately recognized. He filled in on Brooklyn Dodgers broadcasts in 1948 when legendary announcer Red Barber left to work the Olympics. And when an ulcer sidelined Barber, the Dodgers expressed an interest in keeping Harwell. It took a bit of doing to pry him away from the Crackers. In perhaps the oddest swap in baseball history, Harwell was traded by the Crackers to the Dodgers for catcher Cliff Dapper.

A year later Harwell was rotating with Barber on radio and that newfangled medium called television. His sought-after talent motivated the crosstown Giants to offer him a position in the booth alongside Russ Hodges. The pair described to enthralled listeners throughout New York the taut 1951 pennant race between the Dodgers and Giants, which concluded dramatically with the Bobby Thomson home run in a do-or-die third playoff game that gave the latter the crown. Harwell announced that game nationally for NBC, but Hodges received the most attention for his call of the pennant-clinching blast.

Harwell accepted the challenge of making bad baseball sound exciting in 1953 when he began working in Baltimore for the new Orioles, who lost 100 games that year after moving from St. Louis. But a chance meeting in the booth with Birds and former Tigers first baseman George Kell proved instrumental in determining his eventual destination. Kell joined Harwell behind the microphone while recovering from an injury and showed enough talent as a broadcaster to land a job working Tigers games after his retirement. When Van Patrick was canned in 1959 as his partner, Kell recommended Harwell as his replacement starting in 1960.

The marriage between Detroit fans and a beloved friend had begun. Harwell again shifted back and forth from the TV to radio booths before being assigned exclusively and permanently to the latter in 1965. But he gained such respect among his peers that he earned the plum assignment of broadcasting the 1967 World Series for NBC radio. He also a year later boldly selected blind Puerto Rican guitarist José Feliciano to sing the national anthem before a Fall Classic game at Tiger Stadium. The soulful performance, which proved to be quite a departure from the staid "Star-Spangled Banner" efforts of the past, angered traditionalists, some of whom called for Harwell to be fired.

The courage of his convictions drew many fans closer to Harwell, who had been established as one of the premier play-by-play men in the sport in 1973 when he began the longest professional relationship of his career by teaming up with Paul Carey. Critics suggested the two did not get along because they rarely interacted on the air during their stints (Carey described the middle three innings). But Harwell explained that he spoke enough and preferred not to interrupt the flow of the game while his partner worked. And Carey strongly bucked the notion that the two clashed.

"Basically what it comes down to is we have very different personalities," Carey said in 1987. "And I think that's why it works well. I'm a fretter and a worrier. I like the responsibility of the small details. I think Ernie does not. Ernie would like to come in and enjoy the overall atmosphere of the ballpark. Ernie feels that everything is going to come out all right. . . . I've never had a harsh word between us. I don't think anybody ever has arguments with Ernie Harwell. I have a temper. People might get mad at me. But I don't think anybody could ever get mad at Ernie Harwell."[2]

Some might have been peeved that Harwell refused to take the "homer" style of calling games. "I think once you start as an announcer, you have to decide what kind of approach you're going to have," he said. "I decided very early that I was going to be a reporter, that I would not cheer for the team. I don't denigrate people who do it. It's fine. I think you just have to fit whatever kind of personality you have, and I think my nature was to be more down the middle and that's the way I conducted the broadcasts."[3]

That did not mean Harwell lacked excitement when the Tigers performed well. Perhaps his most memorable phrase was reserved for a Detroit home run that he described as "looooong gone!" And Harwell himself was almost long gone as a Tigers announcer in 1990, when at 72 years old he attempted to negotiate a new three-year contract with the club. Team president and University of Michigan football coaching legend Bo Schembechler replied that he and radio station WJR were giving him one more season before forcing him into retirement.

Harwell took the ultimatum gracefully—his millions of fans did not. Included was former ace pitcher Denny McLain, who called the move "classless and gutless." The Tigers faced a public relations nightmare. Harwell landed a broadcasting job for the California Angels and CBS Radio's Game of the Week in 1992 but yearned to return to daily announcing. New owner Michael Ilitch understood what Harwell meant to Detroit, so he hired him to describe innings three to five during ballgames in 1993. So tied to his profession and the Tigers was Harwell that he nixed plans to retire and hooked up with the team's cable broadcasting crew through 1998 and returned to the radio in 1999 before finally calling it quits in 2002 at age 81 following the first season at Comerica Park. So revered had he become that he was honored at ballparks on the road throughout baseball when the Tigers arrived.

His good-bye on the air after his final game, which was played in Toronto, brought tears to the eyes of Tigers fans. Harwell knew his listeners had made it possible to forge the career of his dreams. "It's time to say goodbye, but I think goodbyes are sad and I'd much rather say hello," he began. "Hello to a new adventure. I'm not leaving, folks. I'll still be with you, living my life in Michigan—my home state—surrounded by family and friends. And rather than goodbye, please allow me to say thank you. Thank you for letting me be part of your family. Thank you for taking me with you to that cottage up north, to the beach, the picnic, your workplace and your backyard. Thank you for sneaking your transistor under the pillow as you grew up loving the Tigers. Now I might have been a small part of your life. But you've been a very large part of mine. And it's my privilege and honor to share with you the greatest game of all."[4]

Offered author Bruce Shlain to the *New York Times* upon Harwell's departure from the Tigers in 1991: "Somehow he brings the proper pitch and phrasing to a whole season, with a rhythm and pacing that only a select few have ever commanded. In many ways a Harwell broadcast is profoundly musical. . . . Many an announcer has aspired to sounding as if talking to a friend in his living room, but Harwell effortlessly establishes the same rapport on the air as he does in person."[5]

Harwell died of cancer in 2010. But he could never die in the hearts and memories of Tiger fans and all those lucky enough to have heard him paint a picture of baseball games on the radio over more than a half-century.

CHAPTER TWENTY

The End of an Era

THE TALENT SEEMED TO PRECLUDE EVEN THE NOTION OF A TIGER COL-
lapse in 1989. Lou Whitaker. Alan Trammell. Fred Lynn. Chet Lemon.
Jack Morris. Frank Tanana. Doyle Alexander. Willie Hernández.

But they were names from glories past. Whitaker and Trammell had
both reached their 30s—and they were the youngest of all. For Lynn,
who arrived in a minor deal with Baltimore the previous August, the
greatness of his time with the Red Sox and Angels was a distant mem-
ory. Lemon had permanently faded at the plate since 1987. But the lack
of production from neither Lynn nor Lemon was a surprise. It was the
simultaneous downfall of every key pitcher that played the most significant role in destroying the Tigers.

Morris had won the distinction as the highest-paid pitcher in the
American League in 1987 through arbitration after a bitter contract dispute with the club and was earning about $2 million a year through 1990,
but elbow surgery limited his effectiveness in 1989, and he was never the
same while wearing a Detroit uniform. He compiled a 6-14 record and
career-worst (until 1993) ERA of 4.86. That he eventually rebounded to
dramatically pitch the Twins to a World Series crown proved to be one
of the most inspirational comebacks in baseball history.

The maddening inconsistency of Tanana, which plagued him
throughout his career, continued in 1989, though his 10-14 mark was
more a reflection of a lack of run support than poor performance.

One cannot blame Alexander for struggling in his final season at age 38. But he led the league with 18 defeats and 28 home runs allowed while compiling his worst WHIP in a decade.

Then there was Hernández, the closer extraordinaire and hero of 1984 whose career was coming to an ignominious and tumultuous conclusion. The beginning of the end occurred when he lost his grip on the full-time finisher role in 1987. The following spring training he went all Denny McLain and dumped a bucket of ice water on the head of *Detroit Free Press* columnist Mitch Albom, whom he accused of turning Detroit fans against him. Albom was interviewing Tanana in the clubhouse after returning from covering the Winter Olympics in Calgary when he felt the splash. The source of the anger came from an article written by Albom in which Hernández was quoted as saying, "[Bleep] the fans. I don't give a [bleep] about the fans.... I don't care if you write it. The way they treat me? [Bleep] them."[1]

Two stints on the disabled list with elbow tendinitis interrupted a poor final season in 1989 for Hernández, who allowed nearly two batters to reach base per inning and finished with an unsightly 5.74 ERA. The Tigers released him three days before Christmas that year, and despite his efforts to remain in the game, he never again pitched in the major leagues.

The result of all those collapses due to age and injury was the collapse of the team, which opened the 1989 season at 9-21, recovered briefly in May, then lost 29 of 38 to fall permanently into the cellar. A 10-game losing streak in July and 12-game winless stretch to end August resulted in a 59-103 record on the season, their worst since 1952.

It is one thing to be rebuilding and bad because it brings hope. The Tigers were old and awful. They required an infusion of youthful talent— the more the better. That basically only one young player fueled a turnaround so dramatic that Detroit nearly played .500 ball in 1990 speaks to the level of his contribution. That man was Cecil Fielder.

The massive 26-year-old first baseman who was foolishly allowed to walk in free agency by Toronto after receiving little opportunity to play and had spent one season in Japan became a sensation with the Tigers after a slow start. He slammed five home runs in eight games to heat up in late April. He cranked out six in five games in early May, including one

Closer Willie Hernández was brilliant in 1984 before fading.
COURTESY OF DREAMSTIME, COPYRIGHT JERRY COLI

three-homer "you shouldn't have allowed me to leave" explosion against the Blue Jays. He smashed three during an early June victory in Cleveland. And he was proving himself far from an all-or-nothing slugger as his average soared to .329 by the middle of that month.

Fielder, whose son Prince would two decades later also take baseball by storm for Milwaukee and manage two productive seasons in Detroit, led the American League in 1990 with 51 homers and 132 RBIs and finished a close second behind Rickey Henderson in the Most Valuable Player voting. Not only had he become the first 50-homer hitter in the league since Roger Maris broke Babe Ruth's single-season record with 61 in 1961, but his efforts keyed a resurgence of the Tiger offense, which had finished 13th in the AL with 613 runs scored the previous year and second in 1990 by tallying 750.

Home-run champion Cecil Fielder gave Detroit fans plenty to cheer about in the early 1990s.
COURTESY OF DREAMSTIME,
COPYRIGHT JERRY COLI

He even provided a bit of drama on the final day of the season at Yankee Stadium when he slugged homers 50 and 51 to reach and pass a coveted baseball milestone, after which the appreciative fans gave him a standing ovation and cheered for a curtain call to which Fielder obliged. His sigh of relief could be heard all the way to Detroit. "I wouldn't put anyone in baseball in that situation," he said. "There was so much pressure. Everybody was talking about whether or not I was going to hit 50. This is something I will never forget."[2]

The Tiger revival continued in 1991 as director of player development Joe McDonald was elevated to general manager, replacing Bill Lajoie. A more impactful arrival as a starter was 21-year-old second-year third baseman Travis Fryman, who drove in 91 runs and gave the club much needed protection for Fielder in the lineup, as did power-hitting catcher and offseason trade acquisition Mickey Tettleton. Veteran free agent Bill Gullickson, meanwhile, managed his only 20-win season thanks greatly to tremendous run support.

The result was that two years after losing 103 games the 1991 Tigers even flirted with a division title. They hung around .500 and the periphery of contention into mid-August then won 11 of 14, concluding the blitz with a seven-game winning streak to forge a tie with Toronto for first place before dropping out of the race.

Any optimism generated by that club dissipated in the wake of an 0-6 start the following year that sent them reeling out of the race permanently. Tiger fans had grown weary of mediocrity or worse. The club had finished among the bottom four in American League attendance every year since 1989 and ranked second-last in 1992 despite a homer-happy offense that outscored every rival.

The reason for disenchantment was a pitching staff that had fallen apart as Anderson desperately sent one hopeful starter after another to the mound throughout the early 1990s in a vain attempt to find one who could perform respectably. The organization failed to produce young talent, forcing the acquisition of past-their-prime pitchers such as Mike Moore or simple disappointments, including injury-plagued left-hander David Wells, who did not blossom until he approached his mid-30s, several years after he left Detroit.

Front office continuity had become a problem. Owner Michael Ilitch, who bought the club in August 1992, fired McDonald as general manager and replaced him with assistant Jerry Walker, though rumors ran rampant of a Lajoie return. Walker was canned 17 months later in favor of former scouting director Joe Klein.

Ilitch expressed a willingness to spend on free agents but rejected the notion of handing big bucks to free agent pitchers. And Walker towed the company line. "I'm not going to throw money away," he said. "I don't take the lack of a payroll limit to mean we have an unlimited payroll. To me, it means if we're one player away we should go after him without having a payroll limit to stop us."[3]

The obvious retort was that the Tigers were stuck in a chicken-egg situation. They could not reach the point in which they were one player away from contention until they vastly improved their pitching staff. The only solution therefore was developing premier hurlers in the farm system. And that simply was not happening.

Instead, the team was losing pitchers. The Tigers finally received a healthy and strong season from Wells in 1995 but decided to trade him for a pitching prospect rather than risk signing him to a long-term contract. Among the suitors were the Yankees, who yearned to add Wells to their rotation and, according to the *Detroit News*, were willing to part with promising right-hander Mariano Rivera. But New York GM Gene Michael, who began hearing reports that Rivera's fastball was taking off, nixed the trade. Wells, who had won 10 of 13 decisions for a lousy club, was instead dispatched to Cincinnati for pitchers C. J. Nitkowski and David Tuttle. The former pitched horribly in a Tigers uniform, the latter never reached the big leagues, and Wells eventually emerged as a consistent winner.

The Tigers of that era did spend money wisely on hitters. Among them was Tony Phillips, who arrived as a free agent in 1990 to provide a steady bat and wide-ranging defensive versatility as an infielder and outfielder. After being used mostly as a part-time starter in Oakland, he blossomed as an everyday player in Detroit, providing far more production. Phillips consistently ranked near the top of the league in on-base percentage. He led the AL with 114 runs scored in 1992 and 132 walks the following year. He averaged 100 runs over five seasons with the Tigers.

More important was locking up Fielder without breaking the bank. He was seeking $5.4 million heading into the 1992 season and settled for the $4.5 million offered by the club to avoid arbitration, the richest one-year contract ever signed by a major-league player. Fielder understood why Schembechler experienced a sudden urge to avoid a contentious battle. "He was very adamant about talking to my agents all of a sudden," Fielder explained. "He felt that a deal definitely needed to be worked out. He started feeling, I think, a little bit of pressure from the people of Detroit."[4]

If anyone deserved a huge payday it was Fielder. Though his average dipped, he continued to produce, pacing the AL with 124 RBIs in 1992. He then signed a five-year contract for $36.2 million the next season. Fielder remained a major threat batting cleanup but began to falter. The club traded him with impeccable timing to the Yankees in 1996. Though they only received pretty-much-done outfielder Rubén Sierra in return, Fielder never regained the batting stroke that made him one of the feared sluggers in baseball.

By that time the Tigers could hardly be recognized. Whitaker had become a part-time player as the mid-90s approached despite remaining highly productive, then retired after the 1995 season. Knee and ankle injuries kept Trammell out of the lineup extensively after 1990—he never managed more than 401 at-bats over the last six years before calling it quits in 1996.

Then there was Sparky, who from 1970 to 1988 as manager of the Reds and Tigers had posted just one losing record and none in Detroit. Defeat had taken a toll on the silver-haired skipper. So did the 1994 player strike that forced cancellation of the World Series and threatened

Volatile outfielder Kirk Gibson (right) returned for a less-successful second stint with the Tigers in 1993.
COURTESY OF DREAMSTIME, COPYRIGHT JERRY COLI

baseball with the use of replacement players to start the 1995 season. Anderson wanted no part of it. He refused to manage them, received a leave of absence from the team, and claimed it was all a ruse perpetrated by Major League Baseball. "I managed 25 years at that time in the major leagues and I was no joke," he later explained. "I wasn't going to be part of a joke. That was the biggest travesty I have ever seen in my career."[5]

Anderson returned to manage the Tigers in 1995 after the strike was settled but resigned after that season with the intention of leading another club in the future. But offers never came as some in the sport have claimed his defiance had resulted in him being blackballed. Anderson never managed again.

The Tigers were a mess. Whitaker and Anderson were gone. Trammell was on his way out. Kirk Gibson, who had returned for a three-year curtain call in 1993, had announced his retirement. The offense was terrible. The pitching was worse. And the team was about to plunge into the worst season in franchise history.

CHAPTER TWENTY-ONE

The Darkest Days

THE GOOD NEWS FOR THE TIGERS IN 1996 WAS THAT TRAVIS FRYMAN continued to play like an All-Star and young hitters Tony Clark and Bobby Higginson showed promise.

The bad news was everything else.

Sparky Anderson had before departing stressed the need to develop pitchers in the farm system. The organization had failed miserably in that task and left new manager Buddy Bell with one of the worst staffs in baseball history.

The 44-year-old Bell was hired away from Cleveland, where he had served as a bench coach after having started his playing career there. He was selected by new general manager Randy Smith, who had six weeks earlier left the same position with San Diego. The pair represented the youth movement promised by the organization not just on the field but in the front office as well.

"Coming here at a time when we all can influence a positive new direction is really exciting," Bell said. "The one promise I do make is that the Tiger team that takes the field on any given day will be the most well-prepared and enthusiastic group of players we have."[1]

Preparation and enthusiasm are no substitute for pitching. The 1996 Tigers allowed 1,103 runs, the most in American League history and second most ever in baseball to the 1930 Phillies. They allowed nearly two baserunners per inning and ranked last in the AL in earned run average, walks, and both hits and home runs allowed. Second-year "ace"

Felipe Lira finished the season with a 6-14 record and 5.22 ERA. Not one Detroit hurler recorded more than seven victories.

Amazingly, the Tigers started out strong. They boasted an 8-7 record before embarking on one of the most epic collapses ever. They followed with an eight-game losing streak. They then dropped 10 of 12. They soon thereafter dropped 12 straight and 17 of 18. When the dust settled, the Tigers had lost 39 of 44 before finishing on a 2-19 run and limping home at 53-109 to set a franchise mark for futility.

The lack of pitching talent was exacerbated by the era in which baseball had entered following the 1994 work stoppage. Offense was exploding as many hitters began using performance-enhancing drugs to hit home runs and management within the sport looked the other way while fans streamed back into ballparks. The Tigers played along in 1997 as Higginson, Clark, and Fryman continued to mash, combining for 81

Tony Clark averaged 106 RBIs for Detroit from 1997 to 1999.

COURTESY OF DREAMSTIME, COPYRIGHT JERRY COLI

home runs and 320 RBIs. Second baseman Damion Easley, whom the club stole from the Angels for nondescript pitcher Greg Gohr, added 22 homers and 97 runs scored as the offense grew respectable.

Even the pitchers performed decently. Flash-in-the-pan southpaw Justin Thompson, who won just one game the previous season, emerged as a quite-temporary ace with a 15-11 record and 3.02 ERA to earn a spot on the American League All-Star team, while closer Todd Jones, who arrived via trade from Houston, solidified the bullpen with 30 saves.

The result of all the bashing and improved pitching was a 79-83 record that earned Bell second place in the Manager of the Year balloting. But the Tigers were a house of cards. They boasted neither the hitting depth nor pitching talent to sustain success. An ill-conceived trade engineered by Smith sent the consistently productive Fryman to the expansion Arizona Diamondbacks for prized prospect and fellow third baseman Joe Randa, as well as throw-ins Gabe Álvarez and Matt Drews. Álvarez never lived up to his potential, and Drews never donned a major-league uniform. While Fryman received MVP votes with rival Cleveland after an immediate trade there, Randa struggled so mightily in 1998 that he was shipped after the season to the Mets, who sent him to Kansas City, where his career took off. The return provided a second shot with the Tigers for pitcher Willie Blair, who compiled a 3-11 record and 6.85 ERA in the first of three poor seasons in Detroit. Both swaps involving Randa proved disastrous.

So did the hiring of Smith as GM. The Tigers posted an average record of 68-94 during his six-year tenure. And he embraced the old baseball chestnut about managers used as scapegoats twice in that short period, canning Bell in favor of Larry Parrish in September 1998 and replacement Phil Garner in 2000.

Smith attempted to fit square pegs into round holes upon the opening of spacious Comerica Park in 2000. The dimensions screamed out for gap-to-gap hitters during an era in baseball featuring home-run sluggers, some of whom had bulked up on steroids. Among the power hitters Smith acquired via trade was 30-year-old outfielder Juan González, who arrived in 2000 after averaging 37 home runs over nine seasons in Texas. The trade cost Detroit several players, including talented young reliever

Francisco Cordero, who blossomed into one of the premier closers in baseball for a decade. González, meanwhile, hit just 22 home runs that year while complaining about all his long outs that died on the warning track, motivating Ilitch to publicly express that he was considering moving the fences in to accommodate him.

The owner offered big bucks to keep González beyond 2000 but to no avail. "He's gone," one Tigers veteran told *Sports Illustrated* anonymously in late May. "Look, he already turned down all that money. Now he hates the park, and he's getting booed at home. Why would anybody think he's staying?"[2]

González continued to complain about balls he slugged at Comerica that would have been gone elsewhere. And soon he was gone elsewhere, signing with rival Cleveland after that year and again picking up his power numbers. Meanwhile, Detroit also continued to search in vain for a viable closer after Todd Jones began his descent in 2001.

The club finished strong under Parrish in 1998 to avoid a 100-loss season, even winning 11 of 14 during one September stretch. But they were the same toothless Tigers in 1999 as the successful signing of slugging third baseman Dean Palmer, who blasted 39 home runs, was offset by the sudden downfall of Higginson, who faltered badly before one last hurrah in 2000.

And the pitching remained terrible. Young starters who rose through the organization proved unsatisfactory, though Jeff Weaver provided three decent seasons before a 2002 trade that netted another decent rotation piece in Jeremy Bonderman. Mike Maroth arrived via trade from Boston and proved viable greatly because the team had few other options.

The power trio of Palmer, Higginson, and González, which was supplemented by flash-in-the-pan shortstop Deivi Cruz, allowed the Tigers to approach .500 in their inaugural season at Comerica Park in 2000. They hung around the break-even mark into mid-July in 2001 to offer more hope before losing 27 of 37 into late August and stumbling to the finish at 66-96.

The handwriting was on the wall when Ilitch hired Dave Dombrowski as the new president and CEO in November. The notion that neither Smith nor Garner were long for their jobs if the Tigers per-

Bobby Higginson provided occasional light to some dark days for the Tigers.
COURTESY OF DREAMSTIME,
COPYRIGHT JERRY COLI

formed poorly early in 2002 proved accurate when both were fired after six consecutive losses to open the season. Dombrowski took over the GM role and promoted minor-league manager and Dominican native Luis Pujols to replace Garner and become the first minority manager in franchise history.

"I think everybody will be really happy with Luis, as long as he is here, and I think he'll do a good job," offered pitcher Nate Cornejo, who played for Pujols at Double-A Erie. "He's just a players' manager, everybody likes him. He's relaxed, he brings a little comedy and he's kind of a funny guy."[3]

Detroit fans who cared about their baseball team were not laughing, especially after catching a glimpse at how it played under Pujols. The club lost its first five games for its new skipper to fall to 0-11 and showed little spunk in concluding the season on a 6-30 freefall and 55-106 record. The Tigers were arguably the lousiest team in baseball. The idea that they could get any worse challenged the imagination. But one should not have underestimated just how far their fortunes could fall.

The revolving door continued to spin. A mere 10 days after the season mercifully concluded, the Tigers named 44-year-old Alan Trammell, who had retired as a player for the Tigers just six years earlier and had been working as a first base coach for San Diego, as their new manager. The move was meant not only to tug at the heartstrings of Detroit fans who adored Trammell but also to bring a young and respected presence to the club in a rebuilding phase. He understood the challenges ahead and was not about to boast about World Series championships on the horizon.

"Is it going to change overnight?" Trammell asked rhetorically. "No, we know that. Don't kid yourself. What I'm going to guarantee you is professionalism. That's what I'm about."[4]

One could have hardly imagined the Tigers getting worse than they had in 2002. But they did. For a century since 1919 more than a thousand seasons have been played out by American League teams. And none performed worse than the 2003 Detroit Tigers. A hodgepodge of young hitters combined to finish last in runs scored, doubles, batting average, strikeouts, on-base percentage, and slugging percentage. Five starting pitchers, four with earned run averages over 5.55, compiled a record of 25-77 between them. The Tigers lost an unthinkable 25 of 28 games to start the year, then suffered through stretches of 2-21 in June and 1-18 in September before finishing at 43-119. So porous was the pitching staff that they allowed at least six runs in every game during an 0-10 travesty late in the year.

Trammell and his players tried everything to extricate them out of the morass. Early in the year as a togetherness effort they all enjoyed a clubhouse sleepover. But nothing worked. "We didn't have that sense that we were going to come in and win the ballgame," recalled backup catcher Matt Wallbeck. "We were literally just trying to survive and not embarrass ourselves."[5]

Yet there was a method to the madness. Dombrowski had committed the franchise to a youth movement and was determined to stick with it. Only 100 plate appearances were provided to players older than 30. Not one of 10 starting pitchers used that season was beyond 27. The only old-ster was knuckleballer Steve Sparks, who was released during the season.

Indeed the Tigers began showing signs of life in 2004. Any temptation to fire Trammell under the weight of all the losing and season attendance that had dropped by more than a million since Comerica Park opened in 2000 was dismissed by Dombrowski and Ilitch. They stuck with their kids and began sprinkling in a few veterans to add talent and give the kids a road map to success.

The result was a far superior offensive club. All-or-nothing first baseman Carlos Peña, who had arrived a year earlier from Oakland as part of the "Moneyball" purge, bashed 27 home runs. Shortstop Carlos Guillén was heisted from Seattle in a minor deal and exploded onto the scene by leading the Tigers with a .318 average and 97 RBIs. And a willingness to spend big bucks landed the greatest prize of all in future Hall of Fame catcher Iván Rodríguez, who batted .334 with 19 home runs and 86 RBIs while providing his typically stellar defense and leadership behind the plate.

Rodríguez played a role in transforming the pitching staff from historically rotten to merely bad. Maroth and Bonderman both performed decently as all five starters managed to compile WHIPs under 1.5. The Tigers even won six consecutive games to end June at 37-39 and only five games out of first place, then remained around .500 through July before fading.

Despite the bounce-back some began questioning the Dombrowski plan in 2005 when the club showed no improvement. The lineup featured several high-average hitters who did not produce enough runs to remain competitive. One exception was outfielder Craig Monroe, a 2002 waiver claim who led the team with 89 RBIs.

Injuries gave the Tigers a legitimate excuse for their offensive struggles. Power-hitting outfielder Magglio Ordóñez, for whom they broke the bank in a five-year deal for $75 million in free agency, lost three months to a hernia. Guillén and outfielder Rondell White, both of whom finished the season at over .300, were limited to fewer than 100 games, as was Rodríguez.

But it had also become apparent that the Tigers were going nowhere until they added several viable pitchers. Their starters lacked potential beyond mediocrity, and closer Troy Percival, an expensive free agent signing who had averaged 35 saves a year over nine seasons with the Angels, blew out his arm and performed horribly on the mound in his only season with Detroit.

It appeared heading into 2006 that the Tigers were spinning their wheels. But appearances can be deceiving. A new manager, a budding ace, and a healthy, blossoming lineup were about to transform the Tigers from pussycats to beasts.

CHAPTER TWENTY-TWO

Doormats to Dynamite

IT SEEMED IN LATE AUGUST 2005 THAT ALAN TRAMMELL HAD EARNED at least one more season as manager of the Tigers. They had won five straight and pulled to within one game of .500 despite a myriad of injuries.

Then it happened. A collapse during which the team performed more like the historically rotten 2003 edition than a playoff contender sealed the skipper's fate. The club lost 24 of its next 30 games and five in a row to end the season. Trammell was fired the next day.

General manager Dave Dombrowski proved a bit testy when asked by the media why he dumped his manager. "We thought we had a chance to be a better ballclub," he said before adding, "I did it to him—I don't think I owe it to you."[1]

Dombrowski already knew his replacement. It was Jim Leyland, with whom he worked with the Marlins when that team captured the 1997 World Series crown a mere five years into their existence. The 60-year-old Leyland, who had guided Pittsburgh to three consecutive division titles more than a decade earlier, had not managed since experiencing weariness with the lousy 1999 Colorado Rockies and was itching to return to the dugout.

"I did a lousy job my last year of managing," he admitted after accepting the Detroit job. "I stunk because I was burned out. When I left there, I sincerely believed that I would not manage again. I always missed the competition but the last couple of years—and this stuck in my craw a little bit—I did not want my managerial career to end like that."[2]

Manager Jim Leyland turned the Tigers around upon his arrival in 2006.
COURTESY OF WIKIMEDIA COMMONS

The diminutive, feisty, cigarette-smoking Leyland, who grew up as a Tiger fan in northwest Ohio, provided the franchise with its first respected and experienced manager since Sparky Anderson. But he could not work magic without an upgrade in talent, particularly on the mound. And he got it from one rookie right-hander and one veteran southpaw.

The former was 23-year-old Justin Verlander, a rare prize from the 2003 disaster. The awful record that year allowed the Tigers to draft second in 2004 and snag the flamethrower out of Old Dominion University. Verlander zoomed through the minor-league system. He compiled an 11-2 record and outrageous 1.29 ERA down on the farm while striking out 136 in 118⅔ innings before starting twice for Detroit. Verlander ran hot and cold in 2006, as one might expect in his first full season in the big leagues, but his 17-9 mark and 3.63 ERA earned him American League Rookie of the Year honors.

The other addition that vaulted the rotation beyond respectability was free agent Kenny Rogers. The 41-year-old lefty had proven himself still viable with a 14-8 record and fine 3.46 ERA with Texas in 2005. He managed one last hurrah in Detroit, hitting his stride during the heat of the summer and pennant race in August and September and finishing 17-8 with a 3.84 ERA.

Leyland also needed bullpen aces to lock down victories in an era of a diminishing number of complete games. And he received more than could have been expected from aging closer Todd Jones, who returned to Detroit via free agency to record 37 saves, and flamethrowing one-year wonder Joel "Zoom-Zoom" Zumaya, whose fastball was clocked at 103 miles an hour.

The vast improvement of the pitching staff combined with hitters who managed what can be considered typical seasons when healthy (though the addition of young center fielder and triples machine Curtis Granderson certainly helped) catapulted the Tigers to greatness. They trumpeted their arrival as contenders with a 19-9 start that included winning streaks of five and six games, then embarked on a 15-1 blitz in May that featured sweeps of Central Division rivals Cleveland, Minnesota, and Kansas City and sent them soaring into first place. They continued to waltz through the schedule, winning 13 of 15 in late June to push their record to 55-25. Yet they could not shake the pesky White Sox, and the Twins remained lurking as well.

The Tigers seemed set to roar to the division title after an 18-8 run that coincided with a Chicago slump pushed their lead to 10 games on August 7. But they too were due for a slide, and a 12-22 stretch highlighted by three consecutive defeats in Minnesota allowed the Twins to close within two games of the top. And an 0-5 finish to the regular season that concluded with a three-game sweep to the awful Kansas City Royals handed Minnesota the championship on a silver platter, relegating Detroit to the wild card. The terrible pitching that cost the Tigers down the stretch threatened to doom them in the first round against the American League East champion Yankees.

That fear did not dissipate when the Bronx Bombers bombed left-hander Nate Robertson in Game 1, then Verlander struggled the following night. But a go-ahead RBI triple by Granderson and lights-out performance by the bullpen allowed the Tigers to return to Detroit tied at a game apiece.

That is when the Tigers rediscovered the dominance they had exhibited through most of the regular season. Rogers performed brilliantly in Game 3, blanking the Yankees into the eighth while his teammates were bashing still-intimidating left-hander Randy Johnson for a 6–0 victory at Comerica Park. Then Bonderman, who had struggled down the stretch, rose to the occasion to shut down New York while taking advantage of a 13-hit attack to send his team into an ALCS showdown against Oakland.

It was no contest. The Tigers were clicking on all cylinders. Robertson and Rogers remained in a groove—the latter again blanked a playoff foe through seven innings—and Jones saved Games 2 and 3 to place his team on the verge of a sweep. A throng of nearly 43,000 packed Comerica in hopes of witnessing a pennant clincher, and they got their wish.

The battle was tied at 3–3 with two outs in the bottom of the ninth. Extra innings appeared certain. But Craig Monroe and Plácido Polanco, both sizzling throughout the series, singled to bring up Ordóñez, who had tied it in the sixth with a home run. The fans rose to their feet, cheering and waving white rally towels with every pitch. Ordóñez turned on a low, inside offering by Athletics closer Huston Street and lined it into the left field bleachers. The Tigers had clinched the pennant 22 years to the day they won their last World Series and one year removed from five consecutive seasons of 90 or more defeats. They had lost more games than any other team in baseball the previous 13 years. Now they were set to play for the ultimate crown. "This is what I've dreamed about my whole career, my whole life," said the jubilant hero having a blast after his blast. "I don't even remember running around the bases."[3]

Ordóñez might have preferred a week later not to remember the World Series either. Though it brought winning baseball back to Detroit, the Jim Leyland era will forever be remembered by some Tiger fans as one of missed opportunities to add another Fall Classic crown to the storied history of the franchise. Their team was simply overwhelmed by St. Louis, as the same hitters who destroyed the Athletics struggled mightily against the Cardinals. Polanco was held without a hit in 17 at-bats while

Magglio Ordóñez provided the Tigers with pop at the plate during his seven-year stay.
COURTESY OF WIKIMEDIA COMMONS

Ordóñez managed two measly singles. Verlander lost twice, including the clinching defeat in Game 5 against former Tiger Jeff Weaver. Only yet another shutout effort by Rogers prevented Detroit from being swept.

But nobody could rightfully complain. Verlander dominated the Rookie of the Year balloting, as did Leyland for Manager of the Year honors. A half-million more fans had clicked through the turnstiles at Comerica Park in 2006, and the club was about to reach three million in season attendance for the first time the following year. Ilitch was spending big bucks to keep his team in contention. The payroll skyrocketed from $46 million in 2004 to $95 million in 2007 (and $138 million in 2008).

The youth movement that had worked better and faster than anyone could have anticipated was over. The Tigers were in win-now mode. Only Granderson was under 30 among players in their typical 2007 lineup. Dombrowski even traded three prospects to the Yankees two weeks after the World Series to add 38-year-old designated hitter Gary Sheffield, who proved he still had some pop in the bat and wheels as well by slamming 25 home runs and stealing 22 bases, which tied his highest total since 1990.

But the 2007 club proved imbalanced, greatly because the 1-2 punch of Verlander and Rogers became a solo act when the latter underwent shoulder surgery and finally faded away at age 42. A 14-26 late-season stretch doomed the Tigers to second place in the Central Division as individual achievements took center stage. Verlander had pitched in June the first Detroit no-hitter since 1984 and finished 18-6. Granderson batted .302 and gained the distinction as the third player in baseball history and first since the immortal Willie Mays to record at least 20 home runs, 20 doubles, 20 triples, and 20 stolen bases in one year. Polanco played 141 errorless games at second base as part of a 186-game streak that set a major-league record. And Ordóñez batted an incredible .363 to become the first Tiger to win an American League batting title since Norm Cash 46 years earlier and placed second in the MVP voting.

Dombrowski continued to work feverishly to bring Detroit fans and Ilitch, who was approaching 80 years old, a coveted World Series championship. In early December he pulled off a robbery of the once-again rebuilding Marlins, stealing 25-year-old superstar slugger Miguel Cabrera while shipping out five mediocrities and former first-round draft pick Andrew Miller, a left-handed pitcher with tremendous talent who failed miserably as a starter in Florida before eventually blossoming briefly as a reliever. Cabrera launched his amazing career in Detroit by leading the AL with 37 home runs and adding another 100-RBI season during a string of 11 in a row.

The GM was not done ripping off his rivals. He stole veteran second baseman Édgar Rentería from Atlanta as a one-year rental and heisted heretofore unaccomplished starting pitcher Armando Galarraga from Texas. The former began to show his age at the plate but remained competent while the latter posted a 13-7 record and 3.73 ERA in a one-hit wonder season.

The addition of Galarraga could not prevent an overall collapse on the mound for the Tigers. The biggest disappointment was left-hander Dontrelle Willis, who arrived along with Cabrera in the Marlins trade and continued his downfall after exploding onto the scene several years earlier. His horrible start that resulted in a pitiful 10.32 ERA after five outings coincided with the team struggles. Detroit stunningly began

2008 with seven consecutive losses, rebounded to inch over .500 and close to within five games of first place in late July, then fell apart, losing 12 of 13 during one sorry stretch in September to finish at 74-88.

Some feared the window had closed on the Tigers, and the next two seasons seemed to confirm it. Only weak division competition allowed them to remain in first place through most of 2009, which ended with an epic collapse. They had expanded their lead to seven games by winning six straight in early September, then lost five in a row as Minnesota closed in. A 7-3 stretch to end September fended off the Twins temporarily, but three consecutive defeats landed them in a flat-footed tie with their rivals up north and forced a playoff on the road.

It was a thriller. The Tigers forged ahead in the 10th inning on an RBI double by Brandon Inge, but Minnesota standout Michael Cuddyer responded with a leadoff triple off closer Fernando Rodney. The humbling aspect of baseball reared its ugly head in the 12th when Inge grounded out with the bases loaded and one out, then weak-hitting catcher Gerald Laird fanned. Rodney surrendered a game-winning single moments later and sent the Tigers packing for the offseason.

The late-season collapse underscored the need to add talent. The club had failed to adequately replace Rentería at second and Rodríguez at catcher following a July 2008 trade to the Yankees for bullpen piece Kyle Farnsworth, who performed horribly before bolting in free agency. The Tigers boasted little pitching beyond Verlander—even talented right-hander Rick Porcello failed to gain consistency after a fine rookie year in 2009—and the bullpen lacked depth.

But those who considered the run to a title dead had another think coming. Two months after the 2009 season ended Dombrowski pulled off a blockbuster deal that provided his team with another ace and bolstered the top of the lineup. One of the greatest eras in franchise history began a year later. But it would not have been possible without the man considered by many the finest pure hitter of his generation.

Chapter Twenty-Three

Miggy

The major leagues are loaded with All-Star hitters. Some can even be classified as superstars. But in the history of the sport perhaps only a couple dozen boasted the talent and intangibles to rise above the rest and earn a place in discussions about the greatest of all time.

A few have worn a Detroit uniform. Among them were Ty Cobb and Hank Greenberg. In recent years another has been added to the list. And that is Miguel Cabrera.

Some complained with justification as the third decade of the 21st century approached that the Tigers erred in signing him to a contract extension for $248 million through 2023. But they were likely not moaning when it was offered nine years earlier. Cabrera had given nobody reason to believe he could not roll out of bed and spray line-drive home runs at age 40 and beyond.

Those who watched him perform as a kid in Venezuela would not have been surprised. He is considered by most the greatest hitter ever from that country—quite the compliment given its rich baseball history. Born into a poor family in the northwest city of Maracay, where his uncle José Torres ran a baseball school, he began playing at the age of four. He dominated pitchers in the highly organized Venezuelan youth leagues, which produced so many premier players that they were inundated by major-league scouts.

Cabrera practiced on a diamond next to his home. He joined other kids with a dream. The difference between him and the vast majority of others is that his came true at age 16 when he signed a $1.8 million deal

The great Miguel Cabrera—arguably the finest hitter of his generation
COURTESY OF DREAMSTIME, COPYRIGHT JERRY COLI

with the Marlins, the largest contract ever offered a Venezuelan prospect. His talent had become so legendary that that vast sum raised nary an eyebrow.

A desire to play in one of the American hubs of Latin-American culture lured Cabrera to Miami despite overtures from several other clubs, including the Yankees. Rumors circulated that losing out to the Fish on Cabrera so infuriated easily infuriated Yankees owner George Steinbrenner that he fired three of his Venezuelan scouts.

The Marlins placed Cabrera at third base and tried in vain to practice patience not rushing him to the big leagues. They crossed their fingers on his defense and hoped for the best in the belief that his bat would carry him. His struggles at the hot corner eventually resulted in a move to the outfield, though he returned to his original position when he arrived in Florida before making the permanent switch to first base upon the trade to Detroit.

Cabrera forced the Marlins to rocket him through the farm system and skip Triple-A. His power was last to develop offensively, but he was no singles hitter and was already displaying a penchant for clutch hitting. He slammed 43 doubles at Advanced Class A Jupiter in 2002 to earn a promotion the following season to Double-A Carolina. That is where he exploded. Cabrera batted .365 with 10 home runs and 59 RBIs in just 303 at-bats. He also raised his walk total, resulting in a .429 on-base percentage. The Marlins could hold him back no longer.

The still-svelte 20-year-old debuted on June 20, 2003, in an all-Florida battle against Tampa Bay. Any hope that his arrival would bolster attendance for the perennially poor-drawing Marlins dissipated when a mere 12,515 showed up to the ballpark, but he certainly sent them home happy. After going hitless in his first four at-bats, Cabrera towered a majestic game-winning home run over the center field fence and jumped into the arms of his jubilant teammates at home plate. He had become the third player in major-league history to hit a walkoff homer in his first game.

Cabrera expressed his joy to reporters with remnants of the shaving cream treatment provided as part of the celebration still in his hair. "I feel great," he said. "I feel excited. My first day in the big leagues, my first hit's a home run, it's good."[1]

It felt even better that it helped a team in a budding pennant race. Cabrera ran hot-and-cold as one might expect from a rookie. He moved from left field to third base after a six-game hitless slump in late August, then hit safely in 18 of 22 games during one stretch in September to raise his batting average from .245 to .268 as the Marlins clinched a wild card berth.

The national stage did not prove too big for Miggy. His two-run, tie-breaking single in the ninth inning of Game 4—the last of his four hits—catapulted the Marlins past San Francisco in the National League Division Series. He clobbered three home runs in an epic NLCS against the Cubs, including a three-run blast off power-pitcher Kerry Wood in Game 7. And he launched a two-run homer off none other than Roger

Clemens in the critical fourth game of the World Series triumph over the Yankees.

Miguel Cabrera had zoomed into the spotlight. Some wilt under the pressure and scrutiny of superstardom, but his lighthearted approach to his craft helped him weather rare slumps, and his talent allowed him not only to prove himself perhaps the greatest pure hitter of his time but—unlike other legends who swung the bat like a magic wand such as Rod Carew, Wade Boggs, and Tony Gwynn—one with tremendous power as well. He emerged as a Triple Crown threat every year. He averaged 33 home runs and 115 RBIs from 2004 to 2007 while batting .320 or better in the last three of those seasons. He landed on the National League All-Star team four times and twice finished fifth in the Most Valuable Player voting.

He also outplayed the budget. With attendance in the tank, as usual, team president David Samson complained after Cabrera earned $7.4 million in arbitration in 2007 that another substantial raise in 2008 placed him out of the Marlins' price range. Samson had already hinted that he needed to trade Cabrera, an edict general manager Larry Beinfest repeated to all his peers. He insisted on three major-league-ready players in return. That his team would miss Cabrera's bat was a given. But he hoped to catch lightning in a bottle.

The Tigers seemed a longshot from the start. Dombrowski had developed a strained relationship with the Marlins after having served as their GM. The club worked to downplay the impact he had made building the 2003 championship roster.

The big-market Yankees, Red Sox, Angels, and Dodgers appeared far more likely to land Cabrera. But they fell by the wayside. Talks with the East Coast clubs went nowhere. And though both California teams boasted a plethora of young talent quite distant from arbitration eligibility, the Marlins remained open to other teams joining the negotiations. The Tigers entered the fray during the Winter Meetings. Owner Michael Ilitch desperately yearned for the hitting machine. But Dombrowski balked at the notion of giving up Andrew Miller and outfielder Cameron Maybin, both of whom had been ranked among the top 10 prospects in baseball heading into the 2007 season.

Samson played the three teams against each other in an attempt to maximize his take. Among the names bandied about were eventual Dodgers ace Clayton Kershaw and slugger Matt Kemp, as well as Angels standout second baseman Howie Kendrick. But the GM was enamored with Miller and Maybin. And so were his cohorts. "The reality is that in our room [at the Winter Meetings] in Nashville," recalled Samson, "when Dombrowski agreed to Maybin and Miller, there was an ovation—an OVATION—by the major league and minor league staff."

They were not clapping a few years later when Miller proved himself a poor starting pitcher and Maybin a mediocrity. Neither remained in a Florida uniform beyond 2010. Meanwhile, Cabrera did what seemed impossible—he became even more deadly with a bat in his hands. Despite the incredible numbers he compiled with the Marlins, he failed to lead the National League in any offensive category. That changed immediately in Detroit, where he paced the American League with 37 home runs in 2008.

Cabrera emerged as the most dominant hitter in baseball by 2010. Over the next five seasons he won four batting titles and led the AL twice in doubles, once in home runs, twice in RBI, and four times in on-base percentage, averaging nearly 100 walks per year from pitchers simply too scared to throw anything in the strike zone. He became the first back-to-back Most Valuable Player Award winner in 20 years in 2013. His crowning glory was winning the Triple Crown in 2012 as the first player in baseball to achieve that rare feat since Carl Yastrzemski in 1967.

That accomplishment was clinched when former teammate Curtis Granderson failed to match his home-run total on the final day of the season. But Cabrera felt far more excited when the Tigers clinched the Central Division crown. He was not one to go around turning cartwheels over individual feats. He felt more relieved that the spotlight on him had been turned off and placed on the entire team. "It was hard the last two days because everybody talked about it," he said about the Triple Crown. "I just had to focus; I had to go out there and do the job. The hardest part was to go out there and focus and win games. I said, 'If we win the division, everything would take care of itself.'"[2]

Though the Tigers had edged out the Royals for the title, the fans at Kauffman Stadium in Kansas City gave Cabrera a standing ovation before his first at-bat that afternoon. And when his Triple Crown had become official he high-fived his teammates, walked to the top step of the dugout, and waved his helmet to the fans before being removed from the game and spending the rest of it in the solitude of the visiting clubhouse, leaving some to guess whether he had embraced the spotlight during his run to immortality.

Detroit manager Jim Leyland believed Cabrera only relished the baseball aspect of his experience. "I would say without question he enjoyed it," he said. "How could you not enjoy what he's done if you're a baseball player? I doubt very much, knowing him, that he necessarily enjoys all the extra attention and all the extra conversations he's had to have. It's kind of out of his realm in personality."[3]

The media-shy Cabrera did himself no favors the previous spring training as the focus of attention after a drunk-driving incident after which he refused to cooperate with authorities. He gave cops the finger and even dared them to shoot him. He had two years earlier undergone outpatient treatment for alcoholism after a domestic abuse complaint had been filed by his wife and had proclaimed himself to be a new man. The 2012 incident in Florida indicated that he still needed help. The Tigers carefully avoided the subject that year, but the media reported that he remained on the straight and narrow. He even earned a nomination from the club for the annual Roberto Clemente Award, which is given to the player who best represents the game through positive contributions on and off the field, sportsmanship, and community involvement.

Another obstacle Cabrera was forced to overcome and which made his Triple Crown year even more amazing was his forced switch from first base to third. The signing of slugger Prince Fielder—son of former Detroit standout Cecil—pushed Cabrera across the infield. But he proved himself worthy defensively, committing just 13 errors. That was 10 fewer at that position than he made with the Marlins in 2007, the last time he had played there extensively.

Cabrera returned to first base after the Tigers traded Fielder to Texas before the 2014 season. But he remained aloof with the media, which seemed a contradiction to the personality he displayed with his team-mates and opposing players. He seemed downright jovial with them, even smiling and engaging in friendly conversations with baserunners wearing different uniforms.

One could understand if Cabrera felt even a greater hesitance to be interviewed after he signed the eight-year extension that would not even kick in until 2016 and force the Tigers to continue paying him beyond his 40th birthday. The deal was widely condemned by those who cited its impact on player salaries throughout baseball and a groin injury he battled in the 2013 playoffs that eventually required surgery.

And indeed his production began a steady and permanent decline after agreeing to the contract, which coupled with his weakening production made him untradeable. Cabrera won his fourth American League batting championship in 2015, kicked off his new agreement the following year by batting .316 with 38 home runs, then faltered. Tigers managers continued to place him in prominent spots in the lineup despite mediocre power numbers and declining averages. Beset by bicep and knee injuries, he spent long stretches sidelined or at designated hitter. "I would wonder, why I don't have my power," Cabrera said after a brutal first half of the 2019 season. "When I find out the issue with my knee, I say, 'That's why.'"[4]

Criticism of Cabrera ramped up as his average and power numbers came down while the Tigers descended from contender to doormat. Former standout pitcher Jack Morris indicated that Cabrera was more of a fun-loving man whose personality would prevent him from ever being considered a team leader. And when umpire Joe West not only ejected him from a game for arguing balls and strikes but criticized his leadership skills during a heated argument that followed, Cabrera went off. He held court with the media in the clubhouse.

"(West) told me I gotta be a leader and I told him, 'Yeah, that's why I'm here,'" Cabrera said. "I'm trying to be a leader because it has not been fair the way the guys have been calling balls and strikes. The umpire said, 'Go be a leader.' That's a different thing because I want to be a leader here. I don't want to show people, like, Jack Morris says like he's not a leader. I say what are you talking about? You don't know what's going on here."[5]

What was going on was that the Tigers had collapsed and the fingers of accusation were pointed at Cabrera. Some asserted he needed to retire before his contract expired in 2023 to free up money for the franchise. Others with longer memories contended that Detroit fans needed to appreciate what Cabrera had achieved in leading perhaps the finest sustained run of success the club had ever experienced. What nobody could deny was that whenever he did retire Cooperstown would be calling immediately upon his eligibility five years later.

CHAPTER TWENTY-FOUR

Thrill of Victory, Agony of Defeat

ANY TIGER FAN AS THE SECOND DECADE OF THE CENTURY BEGAN WOULD have needed to be nearly 50 years old to remember when their favorite team boasted a dominant 1-2 pitching punch. Granted, the duo of Jack Morris and Dan Petry in the mid-80s performed well. But not since Denny McLain won back-to-back Cy Young Awards with Mickey Lolich as his sidekick had Detroit owned two dynamite starters.

Tigers owner Michael Ilitch and general manager Dave Dombrowski understood that premier mound talent wins championships and that Justin Verlander needed rotation help. Though they did not land an established ace, they achieved the next best thing. They speculated that Diamondbacks flamethrower Max Scherzer was on the verge of emerging as a stud and snagged him in a trade that also landed fleet outfield prospect Austin Jackson, as well as reliever Phil Coke, while shipping out Curtis Granderson and starter Edwin Jackson.

It was a steal of a deal—at least while the newcomers wore a Tigers uniform. Scherzer justified their prognostication and blossomed into arguably the best pitcher in Major League Baseball while Austin Jackson proved a viable replacement for Granderson, exceeding 100 runs scored and leading the American League in triples twice. He even placed second in the Rookie of the Year voting in 2010. And though Granderson exploded onto the scene for the Yankees, he faded after a few years while Scherzer was pacing the junior circuit in wins in successive seasons.

The swap did not bring immediate positive results. Scherzer had yet to hit his stride, and the Tigers learned the hard way that they simply did not boast the depth of hitting or pitching talent to contend. Painfully young right-hander Rick Porcello never gained year-to-year consistency even after winning a Cy Young Award with the Red Sox in 2016 following a trade before the previous season. The rest of the staff was a mess aside from closer José Valverde, who arrived via Houston in free agency and remained a top closer through 2012, even establishing a franchise record with 49 saves in 2011. And the lineup boasted no power threats beyond Miguel Cabrera. Age had caught up with Magglio Ordóñez, who lost the second half of the 2010 season to a broken ankle and retired after the following year.

Dombrowski believed heading into 2011 that the natural progression of Scherzer, Porcello, and a few relievers along with bolstering the lineup could transform his team into the studs of the Central Division. And he nailed it. He dipped into the Ilitch account and signed two former Cleveland standouts—designated hitter Victor Martínez and shortstop Jhonny Peralta. The duo combined to bat .316 with 189 RBIs. The Tigers also got a bit lucky with 24-year-old catcher Alex Avila, who batted .295 and drove in 82 in 2011 before falling into mediocrity.

One and all played a role in a playoff run. But the key component was Verlander, who embarked on arguably the greatest season ever by a Detroit pitcher. No longer plagued by the inconsistency that prevented him from taking the step from fine to fantastic, the right-hander performed brilliantly from start to finish, compiling a ridiculous 24-5 record with a 2.40 ERA and 250 strikeouts to earn the pitching triple crown. He even hurled a no-hitter against Toronto in early May. That after the dust had settled he would win the Cy Young Award was a given. The bonus arrived when he became the first AL pitcher since Dennis Eckersley in 1992 to capture Most Valuable Player honors.

A 12-17 start coupled with a sizzling run by Cleveland threatened to push Detroit into permanent oblivion. But the Indians returned to Earth, allowing Detroit to hang around .500 through May and stay in the periphery of the race. Taking advantage of weak competition in the Central, the Tigers pulled ahead and stayed there despite never winning more than three consecutive games from mid-June to mid-August.

By that time Dombrowski had pulled off a seemingly minor trade for 6-foot-8 left-hander Doug Fister, who had been plagued by a lack of run support with Seattle. His acquisition turned the Tigers into monsters. He won seven consecutive decisions from August 20 forward, allowing no more than one earned run in any of those starts and posting a microscopic 0.65 ERA during that stretch.

The Tigers remained on fire as they cruised to the crown. They won eight of nine in late August, then 12 straight through mid-September to finish the regular season on a 30-9 tear. Yet many thought they had little chance to beat the Yankees in the American League Division Series.

Victor Martínez gave Miguel Cabrera great support in an excellent Detroit lineup.
COURTESY OF WIKIMEDIA COMMONS

After blasting Fister in the opener, the Bronx Bombers could not solve Verlander and Scherzer as the Tigers held on to win Games 2 and 3 despite the struggles of Valverde. The ALDS came down to a final battle that provided Fister a shot at redemption. He rose to the occasion, surrendering just one run in five innings and taking advantage of two Tiger home runs before the bullpen shut the door. And when Valverde blanked the Yankees in the ninth, Detroit had clinched an ALCS berth against Texas.

That is when the rotation and bullpen that had proven so effective down the stretch and against New York finally faltered. The Rangers punched out the 1-2punch of Verlander and Scherzer, who allowed 16 earned runs in 19⅔ innings in their four starts combined in a six-game defeat that concluded ignominiously with a 15–5 loss during which the latter was knocked out in a nine-run third.

Yet despite the setback optimism reined. The co-aces were in their prime and Fister had proven himself as viable, even potentially dominant. Dombrowski strengthened the lineup by adding power-hitting first baseman Prince Fielder in free agency. The Tigers had added $27 million to the payroll and boasted the fifth-highest in the major leagues at $132 million heading into 2012. They were in win-now mode, and that is exactly what they did.

It seemed everything Dombrowski touched turned to gold. Spacious Comerica Park prevented Fielder from reaching his typical home-run total, but he did blast 30 while driving in 108 runs and posting a career-high .313 batting average. His signing was a reaction to the loss of Martínez to an ACL injury that knocked him out for the season. He was replaced at DH by Delmon Young, who displayed his hitting prowess after Dombrowski had stolen him from Minnesota in a lopsided 2011 deal. Meanwhile, the quartet of Verlander, Scherzer, Fister, and Porcello provided talent and depth.

Independence Day was Wakeup Day for the Tigers in 2012. They arrived at Comerica Park that afternoon with a 39-42 record and fortunate to be only 4½ games out of first place. A Verlander gem in defeating Minnesota launched a 13-2 stretch that vaulted Detroit into the lead. They remained in the race from that point forward but appeared destined to watch the playoffs from home after falling three games behind the White Sox in mid-September. Then the Tigers got lucky. Chicago lost 10 of 12 while their four-game sweep of Kansas City catapulted them back into the lead, where they remained in securing a playoff berth.

That is when their pitching staff made amends for the 2011 ALCS meltdown in a taut first-round battle against Oakland. Verlander overwhelmed the Athletics in two victories by surrendering just one run in 16 innings while striking out 22. His gem to open the series gave the Tigers a critical victory and his shutout in Game 5 clinched it.

Only the Yankees blocked the team's second Fall Classic berth since 1984. And they were clawed to pieces by the Tigers. What appeared to be a perilous path with Scherzer and Verlander still unavailable early in the series proved to be needless worry when Fister blanked the Bombers over six innings in the opener and the Tigers overcame a meltdown by Valverde to win, then right-hander Aníbal Sánchez, whom Dombrowski

Max Scherzer had much to smile about after blossoming into one of the premier pitchers in baseball.
COURTESY OF WIKIMEDIA COMMONS

had acquired from the Marlins in July in yet another rip-off, hurled seven shutout innings in Game 2.

With the co-aces lined up to pitch in Comerica, the Fat Lady was already warming up her vocal cords. Verlander blanked the Yanks into the ninth in Game 3, then new closer Phil Coke survived a two-on, two-out nail-biter to strike out Raúl Ibañez and place his team within one win of the World Series. The Yankees were not officially beaten—but they were beaten. The Tigers steamrolled them in an 8–1 victory the next day powered by a 16-hit attack featuring home runs by Cabrera, Peralta, and Jackson and a brilliant effort by Scherzer.

One could not have imagined the Tigers pulling off an ALCS sweep—of the Yankees no less—six months earlier when they were six games under .500. But those struggles made the fruits of victory taste that much sweeter.

"I just reminded everybody when we took our punches all year, 'You know what? Let's just wait [until] the end, and then if we have under-achieved, I will be the first one to admit it,'" said Leyland as his team celebrated the pennant. "So hopefully we've quieted some doubters now. The guys just stepped it up when we had to."[1]

The steamroller soon stopped dead in its tracks. The Tigers simply stopped hitting against a tough San Francisco staff with the ultimate prize on the line in one of the most anemic displays in World Series history. They batted just .153 in a four-game sweep during which the Giants pitched back-to-back shutouts and allowed a mere six runs. The dream ended in the 10th inning of the finale when closer Sergio Romo struck out the side, finishing the job by fanning Cabrera.

That lopsided defeat inspired fear that the Tigers would never win the championship so coveted by the 83-year-old Ilitch. That concern proved warranted—they never even returned to the big dance before Ilitch died in 2017. But Dombrowski continued wheeling and dealing to try to make it happen. He signed 37-year-old perennial Gold Glove outfielder Torii Hunter a few weeks after the World Series defeat and hoped that move combined with the return of Victor Martínez would add punch to the offense. And it did—the Tigers averaged nearly half-a-run more in 2013.

They certainly provided tremendous run support for one of the pre-mier pitching staffs in baseball. Scherzer had usurped Verlander as the rotation ace in launching a two-year run of dominance that led to the Nationals signing him to a seven-year, $210 million contract after the following season. He compiled a ridiculous 21-3 record in 2013 to win the first of two consecutive Cy Young Awards while Sánchez achieved the finest season of his career by leading the American League with a 2.57 ERA.

The hitting and pitching talent and depth resulted in a near wire-to-wire march to the Central Division title. The Tigers never dropped fur-ther than two games behind and took over first place to stay in early July. A 16-1 midsummer blitz solidified their hold on the lead and allowed them to coast into the playoffs. And when Verlander put the finishing touches on a second straight five-game ALDS defeat of Oakland by allowing just two hits and fanning 10 over eight innings, his team seemed destined for another shot at all the marbles. Though the Red Sox boasted a tremendous batting attack, their pitching was ordinary.

The common belief was that Scherzer, Verlander, and Sánchez would overwhelm their foes from Beantown. That contention gained validity when the latter blanked Boston in a taut 1–0 victory at Fenway Park in the opener. But the series took a disastrous turn in Game 2 when Leyland removed Scherzer with a 5–1 lead after he had thrown 108 pitches. One by one the relievers blew it. José Veras allowed a double. Drew Smyly walked the only batter he faced. Al Albuquerque gave up a single. Then Joaquin Benoit surrendered a grand slam to David "Big Papi" Ortiz. Tie game. The bullpen was not done turning victory into defeat, which became official when Porcello yielded two singles sandwiched around a wild pitch in the bottom of the ninth. Game over. Heartbreaker.

The Tigers did not cave. After Verlander lost a pitcher's duel in Game 3, they rebounded to tie the series behind Fister. But their failure to hit in the clutch thereafter spelled doom. They put 24 runners on base in Games 5 and 6 combined yet scored just five runs as Boston stepped over Detroit to win its third World Series in 10 years.

That was the beginning of the end. The Tigers did not win another playoff game through 2021. The 68-year-old Leyland, who had been working on a series of one-year contracts, quit two days after the defeat, citing a lack of fire for the job after expressing no such doubts during the season and even talking about managing well beyond. "This job entails a lot more than people think," Leyland said in his farewell. "There's a lot more than writing out the lineup and pulling the pitcher. . . . I was low on fuel and I could see it coming."[2]

Dombrowski replaced the venerable Leyland with youthful Brad Ausmus, a former Tigers catcher considered among the more cerebral prospects in the managerial pool during an era in which analytics were changing the strategies of player evaluation and in-game decision-making. He understood the pressure heaped upon him as he inherited a roster still built for winning. Most new managers arrive during a rebuild. He was not among them.

"I'm well aware that you don't generally get dropped into a situation like I will be this coming season," he said. "I understand I'm very fortunate. That being said, I'm not taking anything for granted. No details will be glossed over. I'm not assuming anything going into the job. . . . We're not going to reinvent the wheel here. This is a pretty darn good team. I think it would be foolish to come here and try to make sweeping changes."[3]

The only changes in which Dombrowski was interested were additions that could take the Tigers over the top. He traded Fielder to Texas for hard-hitting second baseman Ian Kinsler, which allowed Ausmus to shuffle his lineup, shifting Cabrera back to first base and Victor Martínez to designated hitter. The GM also wisely signed 26-year-old outfielder J. D. Martinez, who showed flashes of greatness in Houston before that team foolishly waived him. Martinez quickly blossomed into a perennial .300 hitter and one of the premier sluggers in the sport, though his power proved better suited eventually for smaller ballparks such as in Arizona and Boston. The oft-criticized Detroit farm system even came through, spitting out 22-year-old third baseman Nick Castellanos, who emerged as a top run producer.

One and all helped the Tigers overcome Verlander's sudden fall from dominance, which had begun the previous year. He struggled briefly in 2013, then really hit the skids the following May and never recovered.

During one seven-start stretch through mid-June he allowed an alarming 61 hits in 43⅔ innings with 20 walks and just 26 strikeouts while losing five of seven decisions.

Shoulder pain played a role in the temporary downfall, though an MRI that August revealed tendinitis but no structural damage, dissipating his fear that it would require surgery and perhaps even kill his career. Depressed by his struggles, he turned to model, girlfriend, and wife-to-be Kate Upton, whom he years later credited for returning him to emotional strength.

"She was instrumental in me not . . . like, jumping off a bridge," Verlander said. "I was kind of depressed and kind of upset at the world and trying to hide my own shit. I don't like to talk to people about being hurt. As athletes, you're not supposed to. It's an excuse. . . . But she was someone I could talk to. I mean, basically a therapist. Somebody I could trust with . . . worries about my career. Worries about can I make it? Worries about what I'm going through to get back. And just the overall shittiness of it all."[4]

The Tigers performed inconsistently throughout 2014 all year in struggling to fend off Kansas City, which had emerged as a contender a year earlier. Three straight losses to the Royals in mid-June knocked them out of first place, but they regained the lead and remained there for two months. A 6-11 stretch sent Detroit reeling three games behind, but their rivals faltered in September. The Tigers held on for dear life. A 3-0 final-day win by veteran left-hander and 2012 American League Cy Young Award winner David Price, whom Dombrowski snagged from Tampa Bay at the trade deadline, clinched the division title.

Mediocre efforts by Scherzer and Verlander and brutal performances by the bullpen doomed the Tigers in the ALDS against Baltimore. An eight-run eighth inning explosion by the Orioles put the opener away, then reliever Joba Chamberlain and Joakim Soria combined to blow a 6–3 lead in Game 2. The Tigers went out with a whimper two days later in Detroit, managing just four hits to complete the sweep.

The defeat ended an era of greatness for the organization, which was about to experience significant changes at the top and a disturbing number of defeats on the field.

CHAPTER TWENTY-FIVE

A Return to the Abyss

THE SWAP OF PRINCE FIELDER FOR IAN KINSLER HEADING INTO THE 2014 season did not merely land a premier second baseman. It freed up about $76 million in payroll to spend elsewhere. The target for the big bucks was defending American League Cy Young Award winner and impending free agent Max Scherzer, who was about to lead the junior circuit yet again in victories.

General Manager Dave Dombrowski understood that owner Mike Ilitch was no source of unlimited funds. But he hoped the trade for the cheaper Kinsler would allow him to sign Scherzer to an extension. The superstar even expressed an interest in remaining in a Detroit uniform for years to come.

Optimism quickly dissipated. The Tigers released a statement announcing what was reported to be a six-year contract offer for $144 million. The release ominously indicated it had been rejected by Scherzer and his hardline agent Scott Boras, who had long since earned a reputation for demanding every last dollar he could gain for his clients and urging forays into free agency. The organization further asserted that it would not negotiate once the 2014 season began. A terse reply from Boras followed.

"Max Scherzer made a substantial long-term contract extension offer to the Detroit Tigers that would have placed him among the highest-paid pitchers in baseball, and the offer was rejected by Detroit," it read. "Max is very happy with the city of Detroit, the fans and his teammates, and we will continue negotiating with the Tigers at season's end."[1]

Ilitch and Dombrowski seemed disinterested when that time arrived. Scherzer signed one of the richest contracts in baseball history with Washington. That loss might have been overcome by the 2015 Tigers had others in the rotation stepped up. But instead they regressed. Justin Verlander lost about half the season to injuries he claimed years later the club misdiagnosed. Aníbal Sánchez continued his freefall from his brilliant 2013 campaign. Trade acquisition Alfredo Simón proved a huge disappointment and cost the Tigers promising third baseman Eugenio Suárez, who blossomed in Cincinnati. David Price performed well, but his imminent free agency and Detroit falling out of the race motivated a midseason trade to Toronto.

The result was the worst darn pitching staff in the American League and a collapse few could have expected. The Tigers showed no indication of falling apart early in 2015, winning 11 of their first 13 games and remaining over .500 and in the periphery of the division race into early July. And though they soon fell out of contention, they remained respectable into late August. A 2-12 stretch during which only Verlander won sent the Tigers reeling into fifth place and ensured their first losing season since 2008.

By that time Ilitch had either released Dombrowski from his contract or fired him—depending on point of view. He quickly accepted an identical job with Boston, where he later recalled his motivation in his final year in Detroit, including the deals that sent Price and talented outfielder Yoenis Céspedes packing in return for prospects, and his suspicion that he was not long for the job.

"In my heart, we weren't good enough to win it all at that time and that's what I ended up expressing [to Ilitch]," he said. "And I thought it was important to make a decision that would help the organization for the long-term if I was part of it or not."[2]

Replacement Al Avila, who had served as Dombrowski's assistant, was stuck between a rock and a hard place. Like his predecessor he understood both the need to rebuild and Ilitch's wish to remain in contention.

Avila was forced to take the latter approach in 2016 and signed immensely talented, 28-year-old power-hitting outfielder Justin Upton to a six-year, $132 million contract. But Upton had devolved into an all-

or-nothing hitter whose problems were exacerbated trying to slam home runs at Comerica Park. His average decreased and strikeouts increased while his 31 home runs and 87 RBIs did not offset those deficiencies. Spending money on free agent acquisitions to buoy the rotation proved even more fruitless. Veterans Mike Pelfrey and Jordan Zimmermann performed poorly. Only a bounce-back season from Verlander and the efforts of Michael Fulmer, who rebounded from elbow surgery to earn Rookie of the Year honors with an 11-7 record and 3.06 ERA before faltering, saved the staff from complete disaster.

An eight-game winning streak into early August propelled the Tigers to within two games of first place. But it was followed by a 3-10 collapse, and they ran hot and cold the rest of the season in falling just short of a wild card spot. Ilitch died in February 2017, age and injuries took a severe toll on Cabrera and Martínez, the pitching staff regained its status as the worst in the league, Verlander was traded to Houston, manager Brad Ausmus was fired, and a golden era of Detroit baseball was over.

The focus on winning it all at the expense of grooming and keeping young talent, especially after it became apparent to Dombrowski that piecing together a championship club no longer seemed realistic, sent the franchise reeling. Aside from Castellanos, whom the Tigers were later forced to use as a trade piece, the club boasted virtually no premier prospects. Only the promise of high draft picks brought optimism for the rather distant future.

A 64-98 record in 2017 signaled a long slog back to respectability. It also frayed a few tempers. A week before Verlander was unloaded to the Astros, he and Castellanos engaged in an animated argument with Victor Martínez in the dugout following a brawl with the Yankees. Martínez angered the two by playing the role of peacemaker after Yankees catcher Gary Sánchez punched Castellanos, who then restrained Martínez from attacking Verlander. The ugly scene involving two veterans heightened speculation that teammates viewed Martínez as a privileged character whose positive influence had declined along with his offensive numbers.

Martínez lost a month of the season to cardiac ablation surgery after experiencing an irregular heartbeat and retired in 2018. The Tigers had

Third baseman Nick Castellanos performed well for several years before bolting in free agency.
COURTESY OF WIKIMEDIA COMMONS

finally committed to a youth movement despite a distinct lack of young talent. A second straight 64-98 season, this one under highly respected former Minnesota manager Ron Gardenhire, who had replaced Ausmus, provided little optimism. Only versatile infielder Niko Goodrum and third baseman Jeimer Candelario showed potential among the young position players, while Avila was forced to sign washed-up veterans such as Francisco Liriano to fill out the rotation.

That the Tigers could descend any further seemed ludicrous. But not only did they worsen in 2019, they nearly matched the especially terrible 2003 club in futility. They finished last in the American League in runs scored with 582, their lowest total since 2002. They ranked second from the bottom in team ERA at 5.24 and allowed 915 runs, the most they had surrendered in 16 years. Their 47-114 season, which they amazingly launched at 12-10, included stretches of 0-10, 1-11, 3-23 and 1-10. The Tigers failed to win two straight from June 1 to August 9, a period of incompetence that boggles the imagination.

"We always think that it's going to be a steady climb each and every year," said former Tigers star Alan Trammell, who had joined Avila as a special assistant. "That's not how it works always. There's going to be more bumps in the road along the way. We want to think every one of these young kids is going to make it, that everyone's progression is going to be the same and it's just going to take off. It just doesn't work that way. . . . We just have to weather this thing and stay the course and some of these guys will emerge and be really good Major League players that Tigers fans are going to love to watch. . . . I don't know how quickly the turnaround is going to be."[3]

Avila had shed about half the payroll that had peaked at over $200 million in 2016 despite the $30 million still being doled out annually to Cabrera, who by 2019 was a shadow of his former self. The bat speed that once marked his greatness and resulted in consistent hard contact and line-drive home runs was all but gone. Cabrera remained a high-average hitter with a strong on-base percentage but had lost his power by 2017. Those who called for his retirement and other Tiger fans watched with dismay as their team continued to pencil the former back-to-back American League MVP into the third spot in the lineup.

And those same fans who poured into Comerica Park to watch pennant contenders began staying away in droves. Attendance dropped to under two million in 2018 for the first time since 2004 and fell to just over 1.5 million in 2019. Many had grown impatient with the rebuild despite signs of progress from young position talent such as Candelario as well as vastly talented pitchers Spencer Turnbull, who threw a no-hitter in 2021, and Casey Mize, one of the fruits of futility whom the club grabbed first overall in the 2018 draft.

Both the pessimistic and optimistic had one thing in common. And that was memories. Young and old could recall wonderful eras of Tigers history. The great-grandparents could regale their sons and daughters with stories about the 1945 world champions. The grandparents could describe to their offspring how the 1968 title team brought a fractured city together. The parents could tell their kids about the 1984 club that won it all. And even the kids could remember fondly the Tiger teams that came oh-so-close to capturing a crown.

When the present conjures up negative thoughts, there is always the past. And there are the names that Tiger fans connect with the glory years. Cobb. Heilmann. Gehringer. Greenberg. Newhouser. Kaline. Lolich. Whitaker. Trammell. Cabrera. Verlander. The memories of one and all shine through during the darkest days in the history of a storied franchise.

Source Notes

Chapter 2

1. Jeff Samoray, "George Vanderbeck," Society for American Baseball Research. https://sabr.org/bioproj/person/george-a-vanderbeck/
2. "Fitzsimmons' Career," *Detroit Free Press*, September 30, 1894, 6.
3. W. A. Phelon Jr., "In a Bad Light," *Sporting Life*, February 16, 1894, 10.
4. "News of the Courts," *Detroit Free Press*, June 10, 1899, January 10, 1900, 5; *Michigan Reports: Cases Decided in the Supreme Court of Michigan May 2 to October 31, 1900* (Chicago: Callaghan & Co., 1901), 24: 479–82.
5. "Detroit Doings," *Sporting Life*, March 17, 1900, 9.

Chapter 3

1. "'Ee-yah' Jennings to Be Recognized," *Times Leader*, September 18, 2015. https://www.timesleader.com/archive/411256/news-sports-667124-ee-yah-jennings-to-be-recognized
2. Richard Bak, "When the Tigers Played to a Tie in the World Series," Vintage Detroit, November 14, 2013. https://www.vintagedetroit.com/blog/2013/11/14/when-the-detroit-tigers-played-to-a-tie-in-the-world-series/
3. Austin Kidder, "Who Was the Greatest Person in Baseball?" Slide Player. https://slideplayer.com/slide/9867303/

Chapter 4

1. Daniel Ginsburg, "Ty Cobb," Society for American Baseball Research. https://sabr.org/bioproj/person/ty-cobb/
2. Editorial Team, "Six Facts about the Life and Career of Ty Cobb," Imagine Sports. https://imaginesports.com/news/six-facts-life-career-ty-cobb#:~:text=The%20loss%20of%20his%20father,to%20play%20with%20reckless%20abandon.&text=When%20asked%20by%20Stump%20why,I%20never%20let%20him%20down.%E2%80%9D
3. Ibid.
4. Dan Holmes, "The Biggest Myth about the Modern Baseball Player," Vintage Detroit, June 20, 2014. https://www.vintagedetroit.com/blog/2014/06/20/modern-ballplayers-greedy-baseball-always-business/
5. Ibid.

Chapter 5

1. Jerome Holtzman, "Cobb and Speaker Got Themselves into a Real Fix," *Chicago Tribune*, May 21, 1989. https://www.chicagotribune.com/news/ct-xpm-1989-05-21 -8902030567-story.html
2. Charles C. Alexander, *Ty Cobb* (New York: Oxford University Press, 1984), 189.
3. Bill Nowlin, "Dale Alexander," Society for American Baseball Research. https:// sabr.org/bioproj/person/dale-alexander/

Chapter 6

1. Gary Livacari, "Harry Heilmann—Baseball's Forgotten .400 Hitter," Baseball History Comes Alive, February 7, 2019. https://www.baseballhistorycomesalive.com/harry-heil mann-baseballs-forgotten-400-hitter/

Chapter 7

1. Eldon Auker and Tom Keegan, *Sleeper Cars and Flannel Uniforms* (Chicago: Triumph Books, 2006).
2. Charles P. Ward, "Tigers Back in Winning Ways for Series, Mickey Says after Impressive Workout; Grimm Is Just as Confident for His Cubs," *Detroit Free Press*, October 2, 1935.
3. Bruce A. Rubenstein, *Chicago in the World Series: 1903–2005* (Jefferson, NC: McFarland and Company, 2006), 146.
4. W. W. Edgar, "Wild Scenes Are Enacted in Tigers' Dressing Room," *Detroit Free Press*, October 8, 1935.
5. Charles P. Ward, "Detroit Wins World Championship," *Detroit Free Press*, October 8, 1935.

Chapter 8

1. Tom Stanton, "Book Excerpt: Mickey Cochrane's Tormented Decline in Detroit," *Detroit Free Press*, June 18, 2016. https://www.freep.com/story/sports/mlb/tigers /2016/06/18/detroit-tigers-mickey-cochrane/86100246/
2. Ibid.
3. Bill James, *The New Bill James Historical Baseball Abstract* (New York: Free Press, 2001), 452.
4. Dennis Snelling, *A Glimpse of Fame* (Durham, NC: McFarland & Company, 1993), 194.
5. H. G. Salsinger, "Umpire," *Detroit News*, October 7, 1940.

Chapter 9

1. Paul Hagen, "Greenberg's '38 Season Revisited in New Book," MLB.com, May 28, 2017. https://www.mlb.com/news/tigers-hank-greenberg-1938-season-revisited -c232934996

2. Howard Megdal, "Religion Aided a Home Run Chase, and May Have Led to Its Failure," *New York Times*, March 20, 2010. https://www.nytimes.com/2010/03/21 /sports/baseball/21score.html

3. Richard Bak, *Cobb Would Have Caught It* (Detroit: Wayne State University Press, 1993), 85.

4. Scott Ferkovich, "Hank Greenberg," Society for American Baseball Research. https://sabr.org/bioproj/person/hank-greenberg/

5. Dan Holmes, "Remembering Hank Greenberg's Service in World War II," Vintage Detroit, January 1, 2016. https://www.vintagedetroit.com/blog/2016/01/01/remember ing-hank-greenbergs-service-in-world-war-ii/#:~:text=Detroit%20Tigers%20first%20 baseman%20Hank,while%20serving%20in%20the%20military

Chapter 10
1. *Golden Baseball Magazine*, "The Ultimate Game." https://goldenrankings.com /ultimategame8.htm

2. J. G. Taylor Spink, "A Job That Sought the Man," *Sporting News*, November 24, 1948, 4.

Chapter 11
1. Arthur Daley, "Yankee Perfectionist," *New York Times*, April 18, 1969. https://times machine.nytimes.com/timesmachine/1969/07/18/78386827.html?pageNumber=22

2. Clay Eals, "Fred Hutchinson," Society for American Baseball Research. https://sabr .org/bioproj/person/fred-hutchinson/

3. The Gregger, "Fire Gehringer?? That May Have Been the Catcall Back in the Day," Out of Bounds, July 19, 2007. https://thegregger63.wordpress.com/2007/07/19/fire -gehringer-that-may-have-been-the-catcall-back-in-the-day/

4. Steven Goldman, "Breaking the Barrier: Integrating the Major Leagues One Team at a Time: 1947–1959," SB Nation, April 11, 2013.

Chapter 12
1. Hal Middlesworth, "'Need Power,' DeWitt Says," *Detroit Free Press*, April 18, 1960. https://www.newspapers.com/clip/12959290/tigers-trade-kuenn-for-rocky-colavito/

2. Associated Press, "Jolly Charlie Dressen Dies at 67," August 11, 1966. https://news .google.com/newspapers?id=YsQtAAAAIBAJ&sjid=r58FAAAAIBAJ&pg=7192 ,1885290&dq=chuck+dressen+dies&hl=en

Chapter 13
1. Jim Bouton, *Ball Four* (New York: World Publishing, 1970).

2. Bill Dow, "Detroit '67: As Violence Unfolded, Tigers Played Two at Home vs. Yankees," *Detroit Free Press*, July 22, 2017. https://www.freep.com/story/sports/mlb /tigers/2017/07/23/detroit-tigers-1967-riot-new-york-yankees/499951001/

3. Jim Hopkins, *Detroit Free Press*, October 2, 1967. https://www.newspapers.com /image/?clipping_id=22946644&fcfToken=eyJhbGciOiJIUzI1NiIsInR5cCI6IkpXVCJ9 .eyJmcmVlLXZpZXctaWQiOjk4ODQ0ODDQ0NDcyLCJpYXQiOjE2MjAzOTkyNzcsIm V4cCI6MTYyMDQ4NTY3N30.IrIyqGjd0MBbmcIhtM87Dp3C02_OWS4UMh gkTbFiLvQ
4. Ibid.
5. Dick Kaegel, "World Champion Bengals Shower with Champagne," *Sporting News,* October 26, 1968, 8.
6. Bill McGraw, "How 1968 Detroit Tigers Soothed a Rebellious City's Racial Tension," *Detroit Free Press*, September 9, 2018. https://www.freep.com/story/sports/mlb /tigers/2018/09/07/1968-detroit-tigers-riots-1967/1206273002/
7. Ibid.
8. Patrick Harrigan, *Detroit Tigers: Club and Community 1945–1995* (Toronto: University of Toronto Press, 1997).

Chapter 14

1. John Lowe, "Al Kaline, Detroit Tigers Legend, Dies at 85," *Detroit Free Press*, April 6, 2020. https://www.freep.com/story/sports/mlb/tigers/2020/04/06/al-kaline-dies -detroit-tigers/505371001/
2. Nick Waddell, "Al Kaline," Society for American Baseball Research. https://sabr.org /bioproj/person/al-kaline/
3. Robert Shaplen, "On the Lookout," *Sports Illustrated*, May 14, 1956. https://vault .si.com/vault/1956/05/14/43238#&gid=ci0258c0b6300726ef&pid=43238---034 ---image
4. Tom Henderson, "Al Kaline's Biggest Regret? Pulling Himself from the Last Game in 1974 after 3 Innings," *Crain's Detroit Business*, May 28, 2015. https://www.crains detroit.com/article/20150528/BLOG007/150529845/al-kalines-biggest-regret-pulling -himself-from-his-last-game-in-1974
5. Ibid.

Chapter 15

1. Associated Press, "Williams Is Sour on M'Lain Trade," *New York Times*, October 14, 1970. https://timesmachine.nytimes.com/timesmachine/1970/10/14/issue.html
2. Bill Dow, "How Billy Martin Made the Detroit Tigers, and Their Management, Roar 50 Years Ago," *Detroit Free Press*, April 14, 2021. https://www.freep.com /story/sports/mlb/tigers/2021/04/06/detroit-tigers-billy-martin-jim-campbell-bill -dow/7063430002/
3. Ibid.
4. *Sporting News*, "Phils May Reap Harvest with Woodie the Hayseed," March 25, 1972.
5. Dan Holmes, "Billy Martin's One-Day Resignation from the Detroit Tigers," Vintage Detroit, April 17, 2011. https://www.vintagedetroit.com/blog/2011/04/17

/billy-martins-one-day-resignation-from-the-detroit-tigers/#:~:text=The%20incident
%20in%20the%20spring,game%20with%20a%20suspicious%20injury
6. *Sporting News*, May 24, 1975, 11.
7. Joe Starkey, "The 1979 Pirates: Where Are They Now?" *Tribune-Review*, August 16,
2009. www.pittsburghlive.com/x/pittsburghtrib/sports/

Chapter 16
1. Bill Dow, "40 Years Ago, Mark (The Bird) Fidrych Was 'Some Kind of Unbelievable'," *Detroit Free Press*, June 27, 2016. https://www.freep.com/story/sports/mlb
/tigers/2016/06/27/detroit-tigers-mark-bird-fidrych/86420334/
2. Ibid.
3. Thomas Rogers, "Rookie Hurls 7-Hitter for 8-1 Record," *New York Times*, June 29,
1976, 37–38.
4. Ashley MacLennan, "Throwback Tigers: The Storied Life of Ron LeFlore," Bless
You Boys, February 15, 2018. https://www.blessyouboys.com/2018/2/15/17016852
/detroit-tigers-history-ron-leflore-former-all-star
5. Ibid.

Chapter 17
1. Nelson Greene, "Dave Rozema," Society for American Baseball Research. https://
sabr.org/bioproj/person/dave-rozema/
2. Jim Hawkins, "Houk Steps Down from Tigers' Helm," *Detroit Free Press*, September
22, 1978. https://www.newspapers.com/image/?clipping_id=48719733&fcfToken
=eyJhbGciOiJIUzI1NiIsInR5cCI6IkpXVCJ9.eyJmcmVlLXZpZXctaWQiOjk4N
jI0NDMzLCJpYXQiOjE2MjEzMDg3NzcsImV4cCI6MTYyMTM5NTE3N30
.QQW1NoQwrnSCfw2bJxmuyJKFQwPHXv8HW-wktC1Xlmc
3. Bill Dow, "What a Coup: 35 Years Ago the Tigers Hired Sparky Anderson," Vintage
Detroit, February 24, 2014. https://www.vintagedetroit.com/blog/2014/02/24/coup-35
-years-ago-tigers-hired-sparky-anderson/

Chapter 18
1. Bill Bishop, *Detroit Tigers 1984: What a Start! What a Finish!* (Phoenix, AZ: Society
for American Baseball Research). https://books.google.com/books?id=5dcAAgAAQ
BAJ&pg=PA75&lpg=PA75&dq=sparky+anderson+to+kirk+gibson+1983:+%E2
%80%9Copen+the+door+and+get+your+ass+outta+here.%E2%80%9D&source
=bl&ots=EhNRGyrY7x&sig=ACfU3U0YSbHp6YOBgMyuTNBxZcp2w3YGvQ&hl
=en&sa=X&ved=2ahUKEwiL2Y3r7NjwAhUKbc0KHfSQBMQQ6AEwAHoECAI
QAw#v=onepage&q=sparky%20anderson%20to%20kirk%20gibson%201983%3A%20
%E2%80%9Copen%20the%20door%20and%20get%20your%20ass%20outta%20here
.%E2%80%9D&f=false
2. Ibid.
3. Ibid.
4. George Vecsey, "Gibson Justifies Tiger Hopes," *New York Times*, October 6, 1984, 19.

5. Bob Dolgan, "Tigers Rip Padres, 8-4, Win 1984 World Series," *Cleveland Plain Dealer*, October 15, 1984, D1.
6. Dan Holmes, "'84 Victory Parade Was a High Point in History of Detroit," Vintage Detroit, July 25, 2013. https://www.vintagedetroit.com/blog/2013/07/25/84-tiger -victory-parade-was-a-high-point-in-detroit-sports-history/

Chapter 19
1. Dan Holmes, "Ernie Harwell's Ten Most Famous Catch Phrases," Vintage Detroit, June 8, 2016. https://www.vintagedetroit.com/blog/2016/06/08/ernie-harwells-top -catch-phrases/
2. Matt Bohn, "Ernie Harwell," Society for American Baseball Research. https://sabr .org/bioproj/person/ernie-harwell/
3. Ibid.
4. Associated Press, "Ernie Harwell's Farewell after Final Broadcast," November 20, 2014. https://www.foxnews.com/sports/ernie-harwells-farewell-after-final-broadcast
5. Bruce Shlain, "Sound of the Tigers Will Lose Perfect Pitch," *New York Times*, October 6, 1991, S11.

Chapter 20
1. Mitch Albom, "Bucket Seems to Aid Hernandez's Aim," *Detroit Free Press*, November 21, 2008. https://www.mitchalbom.com/bucket-seems-to-aid-hernandezs-aim/
2. Jack Curry, "Tigers' Fielder Makes History with 2 Homers to End with 51," *New York Times*, October 4, 1990, D25.
3. Roger Castillo, "Detroit Tigers Rebuild Reviews Part 2: Jerry Walker," Fansided, September 17, 2020. https://motorcitybengals.com/2020/09/17/detroit-tigers-rebuild -reviews-part-2-jerry-walker/
4. Claire Smith, "Detroit Signs Fielder to a Record Contract," *New York Times*, January 29, 1992, B12.
5. Cindy Thomson, "Sparky Anderson," Society for American Baseball Research. https://sabr.org/bioproj/person/sparky-anderson/

Chapter 21
1. United Press International, "Tigers Name Buddy Bell Manager," November 10, 1995. https://www.upi.com/Archives/1995/11/10/Tigers-name-Buddy-Bell-manager /6310815979600/
2. Tom Verducci, "Tigers Traded a Carload of Young Players for Two-Time MVP Juan Gonzalez, Hoping to Seduce Him into a Long-Term Relationship. So Far It Has Been a Very Rocky Affair," *Sports Illustrated*, May 29, 2000. https://vault.si.com/vault/2000 /05/29/courting-disaster-the-detroit-tigers-traded-a-carload-of-young-players-for-two -time-mvp-juan-gonzalez-hoping-to-seduce-him-into-a-long-term-relationship-so -far-it-has-been-a-very-rocky-affair

3. Gandaily, "Tigers Remove Pujols' Interim Label, Fire Two," *Michigan Daily*, April 9, 2002. https://www.michigandaily.com/uncategorized/tigers-remove-pujols-interim-label-fire-two/
4. United Press International, "Tigers Name Trammell as Manager," October 9, 2002. https://www.upi.com/Archives/2002/10/09/Tigers-name-Trammell-as-manager/6701034136000/
5. R. J. Anderson, "The 2003 Detroit Tigers, One of the Worst MLB Teams Ever, Provide Rebuilding Teams Lessons to Learn from 15 Years Later," CBS Sports, May 1, 2018. https://www.cbssports.com/mlb/news/the-2003-detroit-tigers-one-of-the-worst-mlb-teams-ever-provide-rebuilding-teams-lessons-to-learn-from-15-years-later/

Chapter 22
1. Associated Press, "Tigers Fire Trammell after 71-91 Season," October 3, 2005. https://www.espn.com/mlb/news/story?id=2179572
2. Associated Press, "Tigers Pounce Quickly, Hire Leyland to Manage," October 4, 2005. https://www.espn.com/mlb/news/story?id=2180682
3. Associated Press, "Ordonez's Walk-Off Blast Puts Tigers in World Series," October 15, 2006. https://www.espn.com/mlb/recap?gameId=261014106

Chapter 23
1. Associated Press, "Cabrera's First Homer Gives Marlins Dramatic Win," June 21, 2003. https://www.espn.com/mlb/recap/_/gameId/230620128.
2. Associated Press, "Miguel Cabrera Wins Triple Crown," October 3, 2012. https://www.espn.com/mlb/story/_/id/8458298/detroit-tigers-miguel-cabrera-wins-first-triple-crown-1967
3. Ibid.
4. Anthony Fenech, "Miguel Cabrera Blasts Criticism of His Leadership: 'You Don't Know What's Going On Here'," *Detroit Free Press*, July 8, 2019. https://www.freep.com/story/sports/mlb/tigers/2019/07/07/detroit-tigers-boston-red-sox-score/1668771001/
5. Ibid.

Chapter 24
1. Associated Press, "Tigers Sweep Yankees in ALCS to Reach World Series," ESPN, October 18, 2012. https://www.espn.com/mlb/recap/_/gameId/321018106.
2. Jason Beck, "Leyland Steps Down after Eight Years with Tigers," MLB.com, October 21, 2013. https://www.mlb.com/news/jim-leyland-steps-down-as-detroit-tigers-manager-c63201648
3. ESPN.com, "Brad Ausmus Replaces Jim Leyland," November 3, 2013. https://www.espn.com/mlb/story/_/id/9922289/detroit-tigers-hire-brad-ausmus-replace-jim-leyland-manager
4. Barnana Sarkar, "Astros' Justin Verlander Says Wife Kate Upton Saved His Life during Depression Triggered by Injuries and Career Slump," Meaww, March 31, 2020.

https://meaww.com/astro-s-justin-verlander-says-that-kate-upton-saved-his-life-when
-he-was-in-depression

Chapter 25

1. Jeff Todd, "Flashback: The Spring 2014 Contract Spat between Max Scherzer &
the Tigers," MLB Trade Rumors, April 6, 2020. https://www.mlbtraderumors.com
/2020/04/flashback-the-spring-2014-contract-spat-between-max-scherzer-the-tigers
.html
2. George Sipple, "Dave Dombrowski Knew Time with Detroit Tigers Was Winding
Down," *Detroit Free Press*, July 25, 2016. https://www.freep.com/story/sports/mlb
/tigers/2016/07/25/detroit-tigers-dave-dombrowski-boston-red-sox/87545682/
3. Anthony Fenech, "How the Detroit Tigers Built a Sinking Ship over Four Years,"
Detroit Free Press, September 24, 2017. https://www.freep.com/story/sports/mlb
/tigers/2017/09/24/detroit-tigers-brad-ausmus-al-avila/697075001/